Museums are houses inhabited only by thoughts.
Even those who are less able to interpret them know
that they are observing thoughts in those paintings
next to each other, that those paintings are precious.
Marcel Proust, 1919.

Maria S. De Salvia Baldini

FLORENCE
THE GREAT MUSEUMS

A guide to the main museums and art galleries

EDIZIONI la mandragora

© 1995 Edizioni La Mandragora
50122 Firenze - Piazza Duomo, 9

Graphic design: *Lorenzo Gualtieri*
Translation: Eve Leckey
Photographs: *Archivio La Mandragora;*
Andrea Bazzechi; Raffaello Bencini;
Nicolò Orsi Battaglini; Liberto Perugi;
Antonio Quattrone.
Photocomposition: *Studio Leonardo -*
Firenze

Printed by: Artigraf - Florence
ISBN 88-85957-07-2

CONTENTS

I began writing, as did many of my colleagues at the Department of Monuments and Fine Arts, all manner of books, guides and art-historical catalogues on Florence in the distant 1950's and have continued since then until the present day. It is therefore with a certain degree of interest and curiosity that I follow the latest developments in style and tone which is produced nowadays. With the passing of time, the public, the type of tourist and even the language of communication has somehow changed.

As a specialist in museums who directed the Uffizi from 1969 to 1987, 'serving', as it were, a total of nineteen million visitors during that period, and as Director of the Florentine Department of Art from 1974 also until 1987, I was able to observe this general phenomenon closely. In 1971 I wrote an article on "The Museum and the Masses" (with no derogatory implication for the latter).

In this particular case we are dealing with a written guide which provides us with just the right amount of exact and up-to-date information, and a cultural and artistic introduction without becoming too highly specialized, yet without falling into the trap of generic banality. Instead, the guide succeeds in creating a healthy, well-balanced relationship with the reader. This is a guide which will accompany him on his pilgrimage, for journeys still have something of the ancient, medieval aspect about them, or on his 'tour' like those undertaken by the aristocracy and later the European bourgeoisie from the 16th century until the mid-20th century.

Maria Siponta De Salvia Baldini is an art historian, a teacher at the International University of Art in Florence and at other universities, a qualified consultant who has collaborated on and written many books, a journalist, in short, a highly qualified professional in every respect. With this book she has confirmed the expertise which I already knew and recognized. She has provided us with a complete panorama of the main Florentine museums, a range which is truely unique in the world, with the intention, as she herself states, of being a "silent but efffective guide to many enthusiastic readers and visitors". Here is a text which flows, is easy to read and to follow, and which also gives the latest relevant facts such as the terrible damage caused to the Uffizi by the bomb in 1993.

Thus it only remains for me to congratulate her on her achievement and to join with her in extending a warm welcome to lovers of Florence from far and near.

Luciano Berti
Former Director of the Uffizi Gallery and Director of the Museums of Florence.

Discovering the museums of Florence is a special and unique experience. Everything we see makes us pause to reflect and contemplate. We can almost hear the voice of Donatello while looking at the statues in the museum of the Opera del Duomo, and the ghost of Fra' Angelico seems to accompany us while we walk along the corridors in the museum of San Marco, visiting the monk's cells.

It was not easy, however, to write a guide to the main museums of Florence, considering both the requirements of tourists and possible changes in the arrangements of exhibits. The most famous museums especially, are so large and house so many masterpieces, as well as having rooms occasionally closed to the public, that inevitably, with the limits of time and space, much has to be left out in describing them, just as in visiting them. Today however, museums are filled with an ever-increasing number of people who are interested in culture, yet have little time available. They therefore need a guide which will quickly and easily direct them to the most important works of art, but which will also be a lasting reminder and perhaps unique pictorial record to be studied calmly at a later date. With the aim of creating a handy and balanced guide I therefore decided to describe, in an informal way, those works of art most often presented to groups of visitors from various countries and with different interests, who are on a 'pilgrimage' to our museums.

I have also tried to provide some brief yet thorough information regarding both specific details and overall context which might be of interest to the reader, in an historical account of the museum itself and the art-historical analysis of their collections. Despite their brevity, I hope that these descriptions will succeed in explaining not only the works of art on view, but will also somehow compensate for not being able to see those which are perhaps being restored or which are in temporarily closed rooms. The variety and wealth of artistic expression in Florence is immense and, given the necessarily general nature of the guide, I have mentioned only those works which best represent a period or style, or those which are famous throughout the world, or of particular interest following restoration or conservation.

I hope that this book will be a silent, but effective, guide to many enthusiastic readers during their visits to those museums and galleries which make Florence a unique city of art and culture.   *M.S. De Salvia*

Andrea del Castagno, Portrait of Dante Alighieri.

Filippo Lippi, Virgin with Child and Angels.

for mathematical tools, dedicated to various scientific instruments, now the *Room of the Hermaphrodite*. Next came the Geographical Map room where various astronomical and mathematical instruments were kept, and then rooms of ancient and modern arms of all kinds, a collection unfortunately dispersed by the Lorraine family in the 18th century.

On the west side of the Uffizi were the artistic workshops of skilled craftsmen as well as the Pharmacy where perfumes and medicines were distilled. Lastly, a hanging garden was created over the Orcagna loggia, where the Medici family came to listen to music played in the square below.

When Francesco I died suddenly, he was succeeded by his brother, Ferdinando I. He further enriched the gallery with splendid works of art which he had collected in the Villa Medici in Rome when he was a cardinal. Of particular note is the Medici Venus, a Greek sculpture of the third century B.C. which Gian Gastone de' Medici brought to Florence in the 18th century.

Almost all members of the Medici family added continuously to the collections and, after Cosimo II, Ferdinando II endowed the gallery with the works of art which his wife, Vittoria, inherited from the Della Rovere family, Dukes of Urbino, including many paintings by Raphael and Titian. Equally important were the works inherited from his brother, the cardinal Leopoldo de' Medici who left highly valuable collections of jewels and medals as well as his famous acquisitions of drawings and self-portraits by historic and contemporary artists of various nationalities.

Under Cosimo III the Uffizi again benefited from a new impetus. It became, for example, a matter of great prestige for European painters to be included in the room of self-portraits and new exhibition space was also created.

When Gian Gastone, the last Medici Grand Duke, died, his sister, Anna Maria Ludovica, the Palatine Electress, succeeded in making the famous 'Family Agreement' of 1737 with the House of Lorraine, to whom, with the end of the Medici dynasty, the Grand Duchy would pass. The Lorraine thus accepted that the magnificent art collections which the Medici had created in the course of three centuries should be left to the city of Florence. It is therefore fitting that her portrait should hang in the entrance to the Uffizi. The Lorraine, and later the Italian state, continued the great tradition of the Medici, adding to and maintaining the gallery.

During the 19th century the various collections were separated to provide a more logical and less chaotic organization. Thus the Archeological Museum and the Bargello Museum came into being and the Gabinetto delle Stampe was specifically created for the collections of prints and drawings.

Today the gallery is constantly subject to meticulous repair and restoration and important new works of art continue to be acquired, although many of these are temporarily held in the gallery's deposit, open on request since 1978. When, however, the plan to extend the

exhibition space, known as the 'Grandi Uffizi' project after the Parisian development, is completed, these paintings will be hung alongside those already on display.

Many paintings have undergone restoration or cleaning and these are indicated by a red sticker indicating the relevant date. This has lead to a more precise and occasionally completely new appreciation in terms of art history and colour analysis. Recently, systems to protect the works have been introduced, including glass to protect them from slashing or theft, barriers and alarm systems.

Serious new problems to the organization of the museum were caused by the bomb on the 27th May, 1993 in Via dei Georgofili which damaged the third corridor (rooms 26-33 and 41-45) and the Vasari Corridor. More than one hundred and fifty paintings and over fifty sculptures were damaged. The first statue to be entirely restored and returned to the gallery in December 1994 was the *Discus Thrower*. The sculpture was an assemblage of various pieces dating from different periods and the task of restoration permitted a detailed reconstruction of the various stages in its creation.

The present entrance to the gallery is by the first door on the left under the portico of the Uffizi piazza, arriving from Piazza della Signoria. When, however, the 'Grandi Uffizi' project is completed, the entrance to the new museum will be from a flight of steps in Via dei Castellani.

In the entrance hall is the ticket office and at the far end a raised passageway brings us into a hall which was once the church of San Piero Scheraggio. The church was consecrated in 1068 and was absorbed into the fabric of the Uffizi, continuing to function as a church until the 18th century. Some fifteen years ago however, it was

partially reconstructed and is now the first exhibition room of the gallery. Temporarily displayed here is the series of frescoes by Andrea del Castagno (c.1421-1457), *Famous Men*, detached from the Villa Carducci at Legnaia, and the monumental *Battle of San Martino* painted by Corrado Cagli (1910-1976) for the Milan Triennial in 1936 and donated to the Uffizi by Franco Muzzi in 1983.

The next area originally formed the apse of the old church and fragments of paintings discovered in it are visible here. The first floor landing is reached by the Vasari staircase, decorated with classical busts. Here we see the beautiful doorway, framed in marble, to the old Medici Theatre, where the Department of Prints and Drawings is now housed.

This collection is one of the most important of its kind in the world and exhibitions of prints and drawings in various styles and of different historical periods are occasionally held here. The collections representing the Italian schools, especially that of 14th- to 17th-century Florence, are particularly valuable. One of the most famous 15th-century drawings in the collection is, for example, the *Virgin with Child and Angels*, by Filippo Lippi (c.1406-1469).

Giotto, the Ognissanti Madonna and detail.

Continuing to the second floor, we arrive in the entrance hall of the gallery, designed by Zanobi del Rosso (1724-1798) with busts of

members of the Medici and Lorraine families by Giovan Battista Foggini (1652-1725) and Domenico Fedeli (1713-1792).

The first corridor begins here: the ceiling is decorated with rather fine grotesques, completed in 1581, and the floor which was made in the 18th century to replace the original brick flooring, is in large squares of marble in two shades.

The first room is the *Archeological Room* (Room 1), so called because it is the only room containing entirely antique items. Alongside the antique Greek and Roman marble sculptures are plaster casts of some bas-reliefs taken from the *Ara Pacis*, once kept in the Uffizi. The highlight of this room, reorganized and re-opened in 1981, is the damaged Roman copy in green basalt of *Doriphurus* by Polycletus (5th century B.C.). This faithful reproduction is of excellent workmanship and even the material used has a gleam not unlike bronze, the material of the original. The gallery's restoration workshop is now located here.

The intentionally severe design of the *Giotto Room* (Room 2, the 13th century) seeks to recreate the atmosphere of old, 14th-century Tuscan churches. Among the works displayed are three large altarpieces, with the three famous Virgins in Majesty *(Maestà)*, together representing one of the earliest and most important developments in Italian art. The *Rucellai Maestà* was painted by the great Sienese artist, Duccio di Buoninsegna (c.1255-1318/19) for the *Compagnia dei Laudesi* and takes its name from the Rucellai chapel, now known as Saint Catherine's chapel, in the church of Santa Maria Novella in Florence. It was located there from the 16th century until 1937 when it was moved to the Uffizi for an exhibition of Giotto's works. Duccio had a highly creative personality and his *Rucellai Maestà* was the result of an extrordinary and prolific ability and contains many stylistic elements which he was to develop in his later works. The panel had many vertical cracks and the shading of the Virgin's cape in particular had been altered both by dirt and the oxidization of the colours. Due to the size and importance of the painting, the necessary work of restoration was carried out in the museum. The *Virgin and Child with Saints and Angels*, known as the *Ognissanti Maestà* (c.1310) by Giotto (1267?-1337) came from the church of Ognissanti in Florence and has also been restored. This is one of the few works undertaken by Giotto in Florence after his return from Padua and before beginning work on the frescoes in Santa Croce. This splendid altarpiece, dedicated to the Virgin, is an early example of the greatness of Florentine art. In fact Giotto, although still restricted by the conventions concerning symmetry and proportions dictated by traditional religion, has here attempted some personal, stylistic experimentation and the result lends a powerful sense of mass, depth and severity to the work. The *Maestà* by Cimabue (active 1272-1302), also known as the *Santa Trinità Maestà* (c.1280) was made for the high altar of the Santa Trinità church in Florence and is probably an early work by the artist. The painting is still Byzantine in style, as is clear from the ordered arrangement of the angels and the shading of the Virgin's

Cimabue, the Santa Trinità Madonna.

Simone Martini, Annunciation.

Pietro Lorenzetti, Virgin in Glory with Child and Angels.

dress, but this important Florentine master also introduces some more modern ideas which he too was developing: the figures are less rigid, the child's expression is concentrated, while that of the Virgin is intense and sad. Even the throne, in solid gold and inlayed with jewels, seems to hint at an experiment in perspective, suggesting somehow the end of Byzantine influence.

The Sienese room (Room 3, 13th century) is an exquisite little chamber containing some fine Sienese art. Particularly beautiful is the *Annunciation* (1333) by Simone Martini (c.1284-1344) and its delightful, elegant style is even more interesting and impressive after the severity of the *Maestà* in the previous room. This was the first altarpiece where the Annunciation appears as the main subject in a figurative composition. This work, painted for the chapel of S. Ansano in Siena cathedral, is the oldest, after Duccio's *Maestà* which was on the high altar, in a series of altarpieces made for the side chapels, all dedicated to the Virgin and now dispersed in various locations. The artist was the greatest Sienese master of the *trecento*; of a highly sensitive and poetic nature, he shared, with his friend Petrarch, a deep and fervent love of refined yet vibrant art.

Several panels (The *Virgin in Glory* and the *Blessed Humility*) by brothers Pietro and Ambrogio Lorenzetti (1280/85-1348? and 1285-1348?) provide suitable counterparts to Martini's work. They are clearly more influenced by Giotto's innovations but still demonstrate the detail of colour and line peculiar to the Sienese style. In his most famous work, the *Allegory of Good and Bad Government*, in the Palazzo Pubblico, Siena, Ambrogio develops a concept already found in the *Presentation in the Temple* of 1342, also in this room: he makes use of not only of a form of naturalism which is evident in his execution of detail and the correct proportions of the human figure, but also of elements typical of Sienese art.

The result is a highly personalized style, which was to be the cornerstone of Sienese representational art until the early Renaissance, when the painters Giovanni di Paolo (1395/1400-1482) and Sano di Pietro (1406-1481) adopted the Lorenzetti brothers as models for their delicate interiors and characteristic, bird's-eye view landscapes.

In Room 4, after the small Sienese one, are examples of the *Florentine trecento*. The paintings are still 14th-century, but are Florentine in style, some now influenced by Giotto's innovations, while others have developed in different ways. The *Martyred Saints and Virgins* came from the *Ognissanti Polyptych* (c.1360) by Giovanni da Milano (active 1346-1369), painted for the high altar of the church of Ognissanti in Florence and now dismembered. Also in this room are the recently restored triptych with *Stories from the Life of Saint Matthew* (c.1367) by Andrea di Cioni, known as Orcagna (active between 1343 and 1368) and his brother Jacopo, for the church of Orsanmichele in Florence and a *Deposition* (1360-1365), a panel which came from the church of San Remigio in Florence. Art historians attribute this last painting to Giottino, an artist who was working in Florence during the second half of the century. His style is particularly recognizable for the strong influence of northern Italian art and his obvious delight in the use of

Gentile da Fabriano, Adoration of the Magi.

Masolino and Masaccio, St. Anne with the Virgin and Child.

Giottino, Pietà.

Paolo Uccello, Battle of San Romano.

Piero della Francesca, Portrait of Battista Sforza.

colour and detail which can be seen most clearly in the modern dress in which he has clothed the portrait of his client whom we can see kneeling as she observes the silent and peaceful scene. Note, lastly, the altar frontal (c.1304) of *S. Cecilia*, attributed to an artist who is subsequently identified as the Master of Saint Cecilia (late 13th-early 14th century), for whom we have no precise dates or documentation.

Next is the *International Gothic Room* (rooms 5-6) with masterpieces of the highly refined, European style of art known as late Gothic. The *Adoration of the Magi* (c.1421-1422) was painted by Lorenzo Monaco (c.1370-1423/24) for the church of Sant'Egidio in Florence and the beautiful altar piece, gleaming with gold and lively with colour, is an *Adoration of the Magi* (1423) by Gentile da Fabriano (c.1370-1427), commissioned by Pala Strozzi, one of the richest Florentine bankers, for his chapel in the Santa Trinità church. The artist painted it while on a brief visit to Florence from his native region, the Marche. The superb detail decorating the panel is most skilfully and delicately executed. The flowering fronds seem to burst forth from their background, around the two columns framing the painting and are an

Piero della Francesca, Portrait of Federico da Montefeltro, Duke of Urbino.

Domenico Veneziano, the Santa Lucia dei Magnoli Altarpiece.

Piero and Antonio del Pollaiolo,
Sts. James, Eustace and Vincent.

Filippino Lippi, the Otto
Altarpiece.

Filippino Lippi, Adoration
of the Magi.

example of Gentile's love for natural features. The altar step, with a scene representing the *Presentation at the Temple*, is a 19th-century copy of the original, now in the Louvre.

The *Life of the Anchorites in the Thebaid* on the opposite wall is an early 15th-century work which, despite various earlier attributions, critics now consider to be by Starnina (late 14th century-before 1413). He depicts a floral delight, a magical fairytale world in keeping with the style of the day, restrained, however, by a Giottesque-like influence in the portrayal of the events in the lives of the monks. Lorenzo Monaco's *Coronation of the Virgin* (1413) dominates the wall to the right. This is the only work signed and dated by Monaco who was also a miniaturist and whose late Gothic style tended to be archaic and devotional.

Following this stylistic and cultural development, we now come to the *Early Renaissance Room* (Room 7). The works here are splendid, choice examples of the new style of representational art which came into being in Florence at the beginning of the 15th century, during a period of intense interest in humanistic philosophy, of political harmony between lay and religious powers and of relative economic well-being. The paintings span a period from c.1420-1470 and are described not chronologically, but according to their arrangement. First is the *Battle of San Romano* (c.1456) by Paolo Uccello (1397-1475) portraying an episode in the battle, probably the unhorsing of Bernardino delle Ciarda. This originally decorated Lorenzo the Magnificent's room in the Medici palace along with its two flanking

*Botticelli, the Birth of Venus
and detail.*

Botticelli, Pallas and the Centaur.

Botticelli, Primavera *and detail.*

panels of the same subject. One of these is now in the National Gallery in London and the other in the Louvre in Paris. Demonstrating a daring foreshortened perspective and great artistic flair in the spectacular horses and riders, Uccello's battle takes place in a magical forest of perpendicular lines formed by lances, trumpets, halberds and waving feathers. Restoration has also brought to light the background details, the scene, for example, of the grape harvest at the top and the dog chasing a hare, previously hidden by later repainting. Next is the *Diptych of the Dukes of Urbino* (c.1456-1470) by Piero della Francesca (1415/20-1492). On one side are the profile portraits of Battista Sforza and her husband Federico da Montefeltro while on the other are the allegorical Triumphs, representing the virtues of the couple. The representation of the Duke in profile was dictated by the tradition of noble portrait painting, despite the fact that Federico had been disfigured and lost an eye in a joisting accident which also left his nose misshapen. The background landscape in both portraits is reminiscent of Flemish art, here however its main purpose seems to be to emphasize the isolation of the profile. The *Virgin and Child with Saint Anne* is by Masolino (1383-c.1440) and Masaccio (1401-1428). Masolino painted Saint Anne in an elegant and traditional style, as well as all the angels, except for the upper angel on the right. Both this and the Virgin and

Botticelli, the Madonna of the Magnificat.

Botticelli, Adoration of the Magi and detail with self-portrait of the artist.

child were painted instead by the young Masaccio, with his self-confident use of mass and perspective which can also be seen in the angel with the dress in shades of green. The *Virgin with Child and Saints*, also known as the *Santa Lucia dei Magnoli Altarpiece* (c.1445) is by Domenico Veneziano (early 15th century-1461). Although the artist was originally from Venice, the style of this painting is entirely Florentine from the prescision of design, to the geometric perspective of the landscape and the close observation of light: an oblique ray of sun, pale and clear, illuminates the entire scene with a diffused light, anticipating the art of Piero della Francesca.

Space is perfectly organized in this painting: the artist has concentrated on both the perspective and the proportions of each figure placed within the architectural space. Lastly are two works by Fra Angelico (c.1395-1455): the *Virgin and Child* and the *Coronation of the Virgin* (c.1435), though this latter title is imprecise, as the painting shows Christ placing a jewel in the crown of the Virgin.

The artist is still slightly nostalgic for the delicate detail of manuscript miniatures and of Giotto's later style, yet he paints with a Renaissance maturity on gold background and indeed his devotional fervour and his sublime inspiration make him a rare phenomenon in the early Renaissance.

We can see in this painting to what an extent Fra Angelico was influenced by and torn between, different styles. He handles perspective well, but his figures, although placed in correctly organized spaces, belong to an unreal, transcendental world.

We now reach the *Filippo Lippi Room* (Room 8) containing many altarpieces, all datable as belonging to the mid-15th century, except for the *Coronation of the Virgin* by Botticelli which is only slightly later. All are of the Florentine milieu, apart from two Sienese artists who had, however, many contacts with Florence. These are the *Virgin with Child and Saints* (1457) by Vecchietta (c.1412-1480) and the

Leonardo da Vinci, Annunciation.

Bronzino, Portrait of Eleonora di Toledo with Her Son, Giovanni.

Verrocchio and Leonardo da Vinci, Baptism of Christ.

Virgin and Child by Matteo di Giovanni (c.1430-1495). The principle works are, however, by Filippo Lippi (c.1406-1495), the Carmelite monk who watched and learned from Masaccio at work in the Carmine church. It is to this experience that he owes the sculptural quality of his figures, enhanced however, by crisp, clear colours. Particularly striking is the *Coronation of the Virgin* (1445-1450) which is without doubt one of the artist's masterpieces. After restoration we can see the sensitivity and purity which earlier, extensive conservation work had partly obscured. Today, instead, we can admire its original beauty, the colour glows softly, the shadow-play and the transparancy of the veils give the impression more of fleeting movement than of a static figure. Bathed in this tranquil light, the delicate profile of the Virgin seems almost to reveal a tremor of emotion. The number of people represented here and especially the different expression on each individual face is quite unusual, as too is the fantastically impossible space which forms their setting.

Next is the *Antonio Pollaiolo Room* (Room 9) containing the works of the brothers Antonio and Piero Pollaiolo (c.1431-1498 and 1443-1496). Together they exemplify the preference for a linear style emphasized by incisive composition and vigorous, dynamic forms, so characteristic of Florentine art during the 1460's. Both brothers worked on the *Altarpiece of the Three Saints* although probably it can be mainly attributed to Piero. It comes from the Cardinal of Portugal's chapel in the church of San Miniato al Monte, where there is now a copy and the iconography is related to the decorative scheme of the chapel designed in honour of the young cardinal who died in Florence in 1469. This rather austere painting shows the Saints James, Eustace and Vincent

Giorgio Vasari, Portrait of Lorenzo the Magnificent.

Luca Signorelli, Holy Family.

as rather imposing figures, each standing on a design in the floor and almost entirely filling the pictorial space. In this room there are also three early works by Botticelli which, although they still reflect the influence of the great masters, Filippo Lippi and Verrocchio, hint at the stylistic elements found in his later works. In *Judith's Return* (1470), part of a diptych given to Bianca Cappello by the sculptor Rodolfo Sirigatti, the accentuated and forceful linearity inspired by his master, Antonio Pollaiolo, is clearly seen. In fact, Botticelli worked with the brothers Antonio and Piero on the *Six Virtues* (1469), commissioned from them by the Merchant's Guild, also on display in this room.

Albrecht Durer, Adoration of the Magi.

Next is the newly-arranged *Botticelli Room* (Rooms 10-14). The Uffizi has a collection of splendid works by this artist who so brilliantly interpreted the complex and evolutionary artistic period between the 15th and 16th centuries.

The two best-known works by the artist are, of course, the *Birth of Venus* and *Primavera*, both recently restored, originally painted for the Medici villa at Castello which belonged to the sons of Piero de' Medici, Lorenzo and Giovanni. The *Birth of Venus* is, without doubt, Botticelli's most classic work, treating an allegorical and mythological theme with extraordinary formal elegance. This exquisitely pure goddess of beauty, with light, quivering features, is carried from the Aegean sea by the winds in an almost Hellenistic style. There is a refined and subtle fascination in both the languid sadness of the face,

with its slightly distracted look and in the natural scene around her. The sky, the sea, the flowers cast around everywhere, are all alive with an emotion which anticipates the mood and atmosphere found in his later works. *Primavera* is considered to be the artist's masterpiece and in fact it announces Botticelli's golden period (1445-1510). This painting in particular expresses his aesthetic vision which was the perfect expression of the neo-platonic ideal, generally shared by the Florentine intellectual circles to which he belonged.

The iconographic interpretations are many and uncertain, and now that the work of restoration has brought to light various new details which were previously hidden by dust and the paint of earlier restoration, the work continues to stimulate renewed interest and admiration. It represents, perhaps, the kingdom of Venus described in a poem by Poliziano.

At the appearance of Venus everything around bursts into magnificent flower. Surrounding her are Hermes who chases away the clouds; the three Graces, symbols of beauty, dancing; Love; Spring and Zephyr whose breath blows flowers to Flora. Today the background to the rich vegetation has been restored to the light colours and the original tones and shades, revealing some open countryside beyond the wood. In fact, after this cleaning, we can even identify a very detailed scene which still exists today and is recognizable every spring precisely in the garden of the villa at Castello, for which the picture

Lucas Cranach the Elder, Adam and Eve.

Mantegna, Triptych of the Ascension, Epiphany and Circumcision.

was painted. *Calumny* (1495) on the wall opposite the entrance and *St. Augustine* (c.1490) are both late Botticelli. Chronologically they are preceded by the splendid tondo, the *Madonna of the Magnificat* (1481-1485). This takes its name from the open book in the foreground showing the text of the 'Magnificat' which the Madonna is writing, dipping her pen into an ink-well held by an angel, while she holds the child in her arms. On the right side of the room is the monumental *Portinari Triptych* (c.1475), a work by the Flemish painter, Hugo van der Goes (c.1435/1440-1482), commissioned by the Medici agent Tommaso Portinari, and painted in Bruges.

The triptych was brought to Florence in 1483 and hung in the church of Sant'Egidio. The innovations it represented caused a sensation and it subsequently greatly influenced Florentine art. This can be seen, for example, in the works of Ghirlandaio (1449-1494), also on view in this room, especially in the *Adoration* which the Florentine artist painted for the Sassetti chapel in the church of Santa Trinità. Here, the group of shepherds worshipping the Christ child clearly shows the influence of the realism seen in Hugo van der Goes' work.

Returning to the Portinari Triptych, we can see how important the theme of the nativity was to the artist as, in renewing the world, it enobled the spirit of mankind. The figures are of different sizes, those of men being larger than those of the angels who, on seeing such great fervour, have withdrawn. Also in this room are some interesting

works by Filippino Lippi, as well as a wonderful, though harrowing, *Deposition* (c.1450) by Roger van der Weyden (c.1400-1464), reminiscent of Fra Angelico's painting of the same subject. The emaciated body of Christ is emphasized by the fact that the painting contains few figures, one of whom is an extremely fragile St. John, reeling on the tombstone which also seems somewhat unstable.

This is the only figure in motion; the others are standing in reflective silence. This extremely famous Flemish painter represented a synthesis of the traditional Gothic style and the innovations of Van Eyck and his work was influential throughout Europe during the 15th century.

We now reach the *Leonardo Room* (Room 15). The works here include splendid paintings by Luca Signorelli (c.1445-1523), an artist who belonged to the Umbrian and Florentine schools; the restored *Pietà* (1493-94), painted by Perugino (1445/50-1523) for the church of St. Giusto; two panels representing *Perseus and Andromeda* (1513), and the *Incarnation* (1505) by Piero di Cosimo (1461/62-1521). The works which catch our attention however, are those by Leonardo (1452-1519). First is the *Adoration of the Magi* (c.1481) which was left unfinished when Leonardo went to Milan, displayed alongside some of his early works when still a young painter in Verrocchio's workshop. This picture was a mine of new formal and expressive ideas which Botticelli and Filippino Lippi (1457-1504) were the first to develop. It is one of the fundamental works of the Renaissance, revealing, even more than

Rosso Fiorentino, Moses Defending the Daughters of Jethro.

Rosso Fiorentino, Angel with Lute.

his finished works, the skill and complexity of Leonardo's art. The incompleteness of the work does not in any way detract from its perfection; its fascination derives not only from the sweep of the composition, but also from the figures, the stunned crowd, amazed and overwhelmed, with, in the background, a bloody struggle between two duellists. The *Baptism of Christ* (1470-75) is generally attributed to Verrocchio, but we can identify the masterful hand of Leonardo in the background scenery and in the angel in profile on the left. Next is the beautiful *Annunciation* (1472-75), where the religious scene is depicted taking place outside a Renaissance palace. We can still see some elements of Verrocchio's influence here, but this work is pure Leonardo, and his classical style is evident both in the detail of the small table and in the original way of dealing with the background, allowing the images almost to fade gently away.

The next room is the *Sala delle Carte Geografiche* (Room 16, the Map

Room). This was frescoed with maps showing various areas of Tuscany, by Ludovico Buti in 1589 to designs by Stefano Bonsignore (1760-1834) who painted the names of the areas in gold, red and black. Originally this was an open loggia but it was later enclosed to house various items which were subsequently moved. Today, copies of Galileo's telescope and astrolabe are kept here to remind us of the original purpose of the room, as well as five important paintings by Hans Memling (1435/40-1494).

We are now at the *Tribune* (Room 18), an octagonal room with a domed roof and a wooden gangway along which to walk. In this room is Giorgio Vasari's most famous painting, the *Portrait of Lorenzo the Magnificent*, painted during the first half of the 16th century, commissioned by Ottaviano de' Medici. Lorenzo's power is represented by various allegorical references: to the left, on a marble pillar, he unmasks the image of falsity; to the right a grotesque mask, representing vice, covers a vase on which hangs another rather beautiful mask, representing instead virtue.

Other important paintings here are the charming and perplexed *Madonna and Child with the Young St. John*, (1527-28) by Pontormo (1494-1556) and his equally famous *Leda and the Swan* which has been in the Tribune since 1529, as we can see from the inventory carried out that year. Also in this room are various paintings by Agnolo Bronzino (1503-1572), artist and portrait painter to the court of Cosimo I. Among the portraits displayed here are those of *Lucrezia Panciatichi and Her Husband Bartolomeo*, painted about 1540 for this famous Florentine family; *Francesco I* at the age of ten (1551); *Bia* (1542) the

Raphael, Madonna of the Goldfinch and detail.

illegitimate daughter of Cosimo I, painted shortly before she died, and the strikingly lovely *Eleonora of Toledo* (1545-46), the beautiful and much loved wife of Cosimo I with her son Giovanni. The fine aesthetic sense and the light, yet expert, touch of this sophisticated artist is evident in all these portrait paintings. The *Cherub Playing a Lute* (1522) is a lively and charming work by Rosso Fiorentino (1495-1540) during his Roman period (c.1530), representing his spontaneous creative ability which was particularly close to popular taste.

There are also works by Raphael and his circle in the Tribune, such as the beautiful *St. John in the Desert.* Clearly the work of this great Renaissance artist, it is dated about 1518-20. It was brought to the Uffizi from the Colonna collection in Rome as recently as 1970 and restored in 1989. There are also five statues in this room, including the famous *Medici Venus*, a Roman copy of an original by Praxiteles; it was brought to the Uffizi with other statues and busts acquired by Cardinal Leopoldo in Rome for his villa there and brought to Florence after his death in 1675. The Tribune thus gained three prestigious works: the *Wrestlers*, the *Knife-grinder* and the *Venus*. The *Dancing Faun* belonged to Cosimo III and was brought to the Tribune in 1688. The statues are placed around a magnificent octagonal table, one of the most valuable examples of Florentine semi-precious stone mosaic work, designed by Jacopo Ligozzi (1547-1625) and Bernardino Poccetti (1548-1612) and made in the Grand Duke's workshops between 1633 and 1649.

Raphael, Portrait of Pope Leo X with cardinals.

Beside the Tribune is the small *Hermaphrodite Room* (Room 17), with a sculpture of the Hermaphrodite and the group of Eros and Psyche, discovered in Rome.

We now come to the *Signorelli and Perugino Room* (Room 19). This, and the subsequent rooms, were originally part of the old Armoury. Masterpieces by these two artists, as well as paintings by artists who belonged to the schools of Emilia, Romagna and central Italy are displayed here. Of particular importance is the *Holy Family* by Luca Signorelli, a pupil of Pietro Perugino.

Painted between 1484 and 1490, and probably intended for the audience room of the Guelph Captains, the colours are strong and intense while the figures have a sturdy, powerful stance, as if forcibly contained within the boundary of the circle, seeming almost to antici-pate Michelangelo's works (1475-1564).

Next is the *Durer* room (Room 20) containing masterpieces by Albrecht Durer (1471-1528), the famous artist from Nuremberg. Among these are the charming *Portrait of his Father (*1490), an early work which, however, already displays his own very personal style, and the wonderful *Adoration of the Magi* (1504). As well as other German painters of the 15th and 16th centuries, there are two works by Lucas Cranach (1472-1553): the *Portraits of Martin Luther and His Wife Catherine Bora* (1529) and *Adam and Eve.*

In the *Bellini and Giorgione* room (Room 21) are some of the best works by two of the greatest Venetian painters of the late 15th and early 16th centuries. The fascinating and mysterious *Allegory* (c.1505)

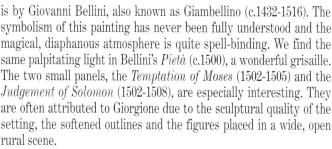

is by Giovanni Bellini, also known as Giambellino (c.1432-1516). The symbolism of this painting has never been fully understood and the magical, diaphanous atmosphere is quite spell-binding. We find the same palpitating light in Bellini's *Pietà* (c.1500), a wonderful grisaille. The two small panels, the *Temptation of Moses* (1502-1505) and the *Judgement of Solomon* (1502-1508), are especially interesting. They are often attributed to Giorgione due to the sculptural quality of the setting, the softened outlines and the figures placed in a wide, open rural scene.

Room 22 is the room of the *German and Flemish Masters*, late-15th and early-16th centuries. Among these interesting northern European works are the *Portrait of Sir Richard Southwell* (1536) by Holbein (1497/98-1543), official portrait painter of the English aristocracy at the court of Henry VIII, and the *Departure* and the *Martyrdom of St. Florian* (1516-1525) by Albrecht Altdorfer (1480-1538). Both these episodes are bathed in an unreal and atmospheric light, illuminating the open countryside.

Andrea del Sarto, Madonna of the Harpies and detail.

In the *Correggio Room* (Room 23) are three significant works by Antonio Correggio. Inspired by the elegance of Mantegna's compositional skills (1431-1506) and by Leonardo's softly blurred chiaroscuro, he succeeded in creating fascinating and extremely expressive human figures.

These can be seen in the paintings on the right, the *Madonna and Child* (1524-26) and the *Rest on the Flight into Egypt* (1515-17). Correggio is not only an excellent painter of natural light and atmosphere, but he also combines elements which are difficult to harmonize; he rarely places his figures in sombre, complex architectural settings, but rather directly into the countryside, as did Leonardo. These paintings demonstrate his interest in the use of light, the mysterious play of shadows, distances fading beyond the horizon, and the sophisticated use of colour. As well as works by Milanese followers of Leonardo, such as Luini (1480?-1532) and Boltraffio (1466/67-1516), there are also two beautiful portraits by the young Raphael of *Guidobaldo da Montefeltro* (1506-08) and his wife *Elisabetta Gonzaga* (1502-03).

These were the Dukes of Urbino who created an active and stimulating cultural centre where literary and political personalities would meet, as described in detail by Baldassare Castiglione in his book 'The Courtier'. Works by Andrea Mantegna, an artist who introduced an innovative element into northern Italian painting in the later 15th century, were brought to this room in 1984.

Here we see the triptych of *Epiphany*, the *Circumcision* and *Ascension* (1463-70). These panels were originally separate and they formed part, with others which have been lost, of the decoration of the chapel in the Castle of the Dukes of Gonzaga, in Mantua. Other works are the *Madonna of the Stonecutters* (1466) and lastly the *Portrait of the Cardinal Carlo de' Medici* (1459-66). The *Miniatures Room* (Room 24) ends the suite of rooms along the first corridor. Some of the 472 miniature portraits belonging to the Uffizi are displayed here.

Pontormo, the Supper at Emmaus.

This is the second largest collection in the world, after that of the Victoria and Albert Museum in London and is of considerable importance both for the quality of the paintings and the period of time they cover, from the end of the 15th to the mid-18th centuries. Particularly delightful are the fourteen oval miniatures of *Henry II of Valois and His Family* (c.1510) by François Clouet (1475/80-1541). Displayed above the portraits are six of the most important parchments from the collection of some 250.

Leaving this room, we come to the the second corridor linking the two longer ones. From its double row of windows there is a splendid view of the Arno, Ponte Vecchio and the Vasari corridor. Some Roman sculptures are displayed here.

We now come to the third corridor of the gallery. The red brick floors both here and in the second corridor were re-made during the course of this century, while the splendidly decorated vaulted ceilings are original. This corridor which, like the others, houses antique statues, leads to the terrace above the Loggia dei Lanzi, once a hanging garden. The second door on the left leads to the Vasari Corridor, open only on appointment for group visits after its recent restoration.

Titian, the Urbino Venus.

Parmigianino, Virgin of the Long Neck.

Displayed in the corridor are over seven hundred works including some from the 17th and 18th centuries. It also houses much of the important collection of self-portraits which was recently enhanced by the addition of over more than two hundred self-portraits of modern and contemporary artists. There are also separate German, Flemish, Dutch, French and English sections. The Vasari Corridor is open to the public as far as the Boboli Gardens and in the last section is the *Iconographic Collection*, portraying a wide range of historical personalities from the 16th to the 19th centuries.

We now arrive at the *Michelangelo Room* (Room 25) with the splendid *Holy Family*, painted by Michelangelo between 1506 and 1508 for the wealthy merchant Agnolo Doni, from whom it takes the name the *Doni Tondo*. This masterpiece is the only confirmed panel painting by the artist and it reveals his grandiose concept of form, space, tension and mass, as if affirming the superiority of sculpture over painting. His forms have, in fact, the same internal dynamism as his sculptures while, after restoration, the colours have assumed a lightness, clarity, and a rare jewel-like quality. Another painting, also important for the use of colour and the expression of movement, is displayed in this room: *Moses Defending the Daughters of Jethro* (1523) by Rosso Fiorentino, one of the best and most fascinating works by this Florentine Mannerist painter. This painting is of particular importance for the treatment of space, ignoring the mathematical rules of perspective and using instead a kind of sculptural layering of the figures to create a sense of both height and depth. The *Vision of St.*

Bernard, a masterpiece by Fra Bartolomeo (1472-1517) is based on a quite different and clearly devotional concept of art and painting, which recent restoration has made easier to appreciate. Also in this room are works by his assistant, Mariotto Albertinelli (1474-1515). On the left wall are *Salome* (c.1515) and the *Virgin and Child* (1517) by the Spanish sculptor and painter Alonso Berruguete (c.1486-1561), son of the more famous artist Pedro. Inspired by Michelangelo's cartoon of the *Battle of Cascina* while in Florence, he remained influenced by the structural power of Italian art for a considerable period and introduced it not only into his rare paintings, but also into his more numerous sculptures.

In the next room, the *Raphael and Andrea del Sarto Room* (26) we have examples from the artistic ambience of Urbino. The *Portrait of an Unknown Man*, generally believed to be *Francesco Maria della Rovere* (1503-04) is early 16th-century. The *Virgin of the Goldfinch* (1505-06), painted for Lorenzo Nasi, was damaged as can still be seen despite restoration, in 1547 when the palace in which it was housed collapsed. We can see the influence of Leonardo and Michelangelo in this painting, the preparatory sketch of which is in the Ashmolean Museum, Oxford.

Sebastiano del Piombo, the Death of Adonis.

Lorenzo Lotto, the Chastity of Susanna.

The signature of the self portrait which follows has been confirmed after scientific tests and the portraits of *Giulio II* (1512) and *Leo X with the Cardinals Giulio de' Medici and Luigi de' Rossi* (1518) are later paintings by the artist, influenced by Flemish and Venetian portrait painting. In the latter portrait the importance, social standing and cultural interests of the Medici pope are emphasized and symbolized by an illuminated book while, impressively flanked by two cardinals, his dignity is exalted by this triumphal show of red. A correct and complete interpretation of the famous *Madonna of the Harpies* (1517) by Andrea del Sarto (1486-1530), has been made possible by recent restoration. The works by Pontormo here are a foretaste of the next room.

Room 27 is the *Pontormo and Rosso Fiorentino Room*, the two most original students of Andrea del Sarto, known as the 'perfect painter'. Displayed here are masterpieces by these two great exponents of Tuscan Mannerism. Pontormo was the more original and sophisticated artist and immediately on the right we see his *Supper at Emmaus* painted in 1525 (the date can be seen on the scroll in the bottom right corner) for the Carthusian monks of San Lorenzo at Galluzzo. Pontormo took refuge from the plague there where we can still see his frescoes with Stories from the Passion, inspired by Durer's woodcuts. His art is anguished, cerebral and introspective, an element which he clearly derived from northern influences. We can sense this even in his classically traditional portraits: *Maria Salviati* (1543) for example, the wife of Giovanni delle Bande Nere and mother of the future Cosimo I de' Medici, seems to communicate a feeling of bewilderment and slight apprehension.

Immediately facing the entrance to the room, on the left, the *Portrait of a Young Girl* (1514) and the *Madonna and Saints* (c.1518) are two

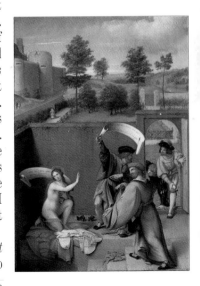

Veronese, Holy Family with Sts. Barbara and John.

Annibale Carracci, Venus with Satyrs and Cupids.

highly individual works by Rosso Fiorentino who was also obsessed by the tormenting problems of form and colour. The *Holy Family*, known as *Panciatichi* (1540) is by Agnolo Bronzino. A pupil of Pontormo, he developed his teacher's representational theories, but restrained them within precise, controlled limits, rigidly trying to restrain any emotion, both in his religious subjects and in his more skillfully

Rubens, Portrait of Isabella Brandt.

executed portraits.

The *Titian Room* (Room 28) is the first in the gallery dedicated to Venetian Renaissance painting. Looking around the room we are immediately aware of a new atmosphere, quite different to that of the previous rooms of Tuscan painting. The desperate quest to achieve a linear quality, the compositions created in cold colours, give way here to a greater naturalism in the figures, and the light assumes a warm glow. *Flora*, a youthful work by Titian (c.1490-1576) was once believed to be a portrait of Violante, daughter of Palma il Vecchio, though it is more probably a representation of the mythical goddess. She is a typical example of Titian's female type, softly sensual and slightly dreamy. His famous *Venus* (1538), also known as the *Venus of Urbino* as it belonged to Guidobaldo, Duke of Urbino, is a splendid female nude, rendered more sensual by the subtle and even slightly provoca- tive silky gleam of the material on which she lies. There are also three important portraits by this great artist, as well as other examples of Venetian art, in particular works by Iacopo Palma il Vecchio (c.1480- 1528), one of the leading exponents of Giorgione's Venetian style of art.

Next on our artistic itinerary (Room 29) is the *Parmigianino Room*, with works by this leading central Italian Mannerist. There are many examples of the work of this artist and others of the same school and style in this and the following rooms. The famous *Virgin and Child*

with Angels also known as the *Virgin of the Long Neck* (1534-40) is Parmigianino's masterpiece in which he developed a refined style, creating an unusually elongated and supple human form, which we see again in the *Virgin and Child with Saints (the San Zaccaria Virgin)*, an earlier work. The image of the Virgin is of rare beauty, clearly of more profound and intellectual inspiration than religious and spontaneous.

The *Emilian Study* (Room 30) is a small room where the works of various artists of the Emilian Mannerist school are displayed. Although all from the same area, their styles were quite different and individual as can be seen from the *Portrait of a Young Man* by Niccolò del Abate (c.1512-1571) and the *Virgin and Child with Saints* by Ludovico Mazzolino (c.1480-1528).

The *Dosso Dossi Room* (Room 31) houses the famous *Witchcraft* by this exuberant and highly imaginative painter from Ferrara (c.1489-1542). It is somewhat difficult to interpret the iconographic meaning of this work though it may, perhaps, represent a magic ritual at which courtiers and gentlemen assist. Beside is the *Portrait of a Lady*, also known as the *Fornarina* by the Venetian Sebastiano del Piombo (c.1485-1547).

The quality of the colour in this painting has been enhanced by careful cleaning, revealing the splendid velvety blue of the material and the intense green of the background.

We now come to the *Sebastiano del Piombo and Lorenzo Lotto Room* (Room 32) which is also dedicated to 16th-century Venetian artists. Of particular importance is the large painting of the *Death of Adonis* by Sebastiano del Piombo. The style of the nudes in the foreground reveals the influence of Michelangelo but the artistic concepts, developed by Giorgione, of achieving impact and exploiting colour are

Caravaggio, Bacchus.

Caravaggio, the Sacrifice of Isaac.

also evident. The two works by Lotto, the *Holy Family* (1534) and *Susanna and the Elders* (1517) demonstrate his fervid imagination and his ability to unite aspects of Leonardo and Raphael thus creating a disturbing and quite individual style.

The *Corridor of the Cinquecento* (Room 33) is a small passage where many late 16th-century European paintings, all Mannerist in style, are displayed. This leads into the next room where the collection of Venetian paintings continues.

The works in the *Veronese Room* (Room 34) are the ultimate expression of Venetian Renaissance culture. The *Holy Family with St. Barbara* is a splendid painting, a marvel of light and tranquillity with clear, crisp colours and sharp, transparant shadows, emphasizing the figures, their clothing and their surroundings. In addition to this and other paintings by Veronese, are works by Giovan Battista Moroni (c.1520-1578), a painter from Bergamo, active during the mid-16th century, whose colour tones and romantic style were more sombre and tranquil. Although clearly a follower of the northern school of naturalism, he was, more than anything, a portrait painter. In contrast to Bronzino who painted almost exclusively the rich, aristocratic social classes, Moroni was also interested in ordinary people such as craftsmen (a famous example is his painting the *Tailor* in the National Gallery, London) and the professional classes. He thus prepared the way for Caravaggio who began his artistic career painting similar subjects.

Rembrandt, Portrait of an Old Man.

Leaving this room, with the entrance to the Vasari corridor on our right, we enter the large *Barocci and Tintoretto Room* (Room 35). Reorganized in the early 1950's, the paintings here complete this fascinating panorama of 16th-century Venetian art. Some of Tintoretto's (1518-94) most famous works are here and a close study of them enables us to appreciate his artistic philosophy.

Leda, for example, is a late work and the artist's vibrant design is defined with decisive brush-strokes and a tortuous style, while the composition has an unusual perspective and a crepuscular and artificial atmosphere. These elements, with their heavy, dark colours and occasional flashes of light are common to all of Tintoretto's works. The art form which most interested him was the nude and he succeeded in adapting Michelangelo's exuberant style of portraying it to Mannerism, leaving us many wonderful examples of the genre.

Other works here are by Bassano (c.1517-1592) and his school, and Federico Barocci (1528/35-1612) from Urbino is represented with several excellent paintings. Of particular interest is the *Madonna of the People* (1579) of which there remain numerous preparatory drawings, demonstrating the immense effort which went into its creation. This is a fundamental work not only to our understanding of the artist, but also because it became an important model for devotional art whose influence was extensive during most of the 17th century. In quite a different style is the recently-acquired *Sts. John the Evangelist and Francis* (c.1600) by El Greco (1541-1614), with its alluring mysticism and almost deformed figures expressing languid pathos.

Passing through the exit hall, we come to the *Rubens Room* (Room 41) decorated in rich, warm red and dedicated to one of the most important artists of the Baroque period. The room also contains works by Van Dyck (1599-1641) and other contemporaries and pupils. Two of Rubens most interesting works here represent events in the life of Henry IV of France: the *Triumphal Entry of Henry IV* and *Henry IV at the Battle of Ivry*, painted for his wife, Maria de' Medici after 1625. Although incomplete, they lack none of the narrative and colourful impact typical of the master. The charm of the beautiful *Portrait of Isabella Brandt*, the artist's first wife, is more gentle and intimate, however. Her features, combining softness and intelligence, familiarity and sensuality, reveal the painter's great affection for his subject. Lastly are some beautiful portraits by Van Dyck, which, although formal, do not lack in emotional energy, as is obvious from that of Margaret of Lorraine, Duchess of Orleans.

The *Room of Niobe* (Room 42) takes its name from the group of sculptures, dated between 150 and 100 B.C., representing the myth of Niobe, the mother whose children were so beautiful that she wanted to place them before those of Apollo and Diana, thus causing them to be killed by arrows fired from the winged chariots of the two gods. This Neo-classical room was designed by Gaspare Maria Paoletti (1727-1813). It is an interesting example of an 18th-century interior planned for artistic display, as it was commissioned specifically by Grand Duke Pietro Leopoldo to provide a suitable setting for this group of sculptures, discovered in Rome in 1583 and brought to Florence in 1775. Also in this room is the beautiful neo-Attic Medici vase, brought from the Villa Medici in Rome. From the 1700's on, a vast number of copies of this vase were made to adorn the gardens of important aristocratic villas. With the *Caravaggio Room* (Room 43) we begin the collection of 17th-century paintings. This is continued in the first part of the Vasari Corridor and represents the continuing interest of the Medici family in new artistic developments. The foremost painters of the two artistic movements of the 17th century, Caravaggio (1571-1610) and Annibale Carraci (1560-1609), are displayed here. Caracci was one of the founders of the Bologna school known as the 'Incamminati'. Their classic ideals were represented by the cult of Dionysus in euphoric, bacchanalian scenes with satyrs, which became idyllic within their rural settings, as for example, in the early *Venus with Satyrs and Cupids*. There are also works by other members of the Bologna school, such as Giovan Francesco Barbieri, known as Guercino (1591-1666) and Francesco Albani (1578-1660). Particularly interesting are the delightful *Angel's Head* by Gian Lorenzo Bernini (1598-1680), the famous sculptor whose activity as a painter is little known even today, and the *Seascape* by Claude Lorrain (1600-1682), which the great French landscape painter completed in 1637 in Rome for Cardinal Carlo de' Medici.

There are several works by Caravaggio here. The juvenile work, *Bacchus*, still uses bright, luminous colours, but the casual introduc-

Artemisia Gentileschi, Judith and Holopherne.

tion of a still life as an exercise in itself, is an innovation. More than anything it would seem that the artist's real intention was to paint the fruits of autumn in all their sculptural detail, with the greatest possible skill. The *Sacrifice of Isaac* has a precise and elegant composition, a refined and original interpretation of a traditional theme. The truly innovative element is provided by the light, however. From a shadowy base the image is highlighted by a powerful and dazzliing light, giving vigorous form to the volumetric space, and thus providing new artistic ideas and inspiration for European art.

Room 44 is the *Rembrandt and Flemish Room*, which also includes many northern European works. The artistic skill and moral stature of the great 17th-century Dutch painter, Rembrandt (1606-1669) dominate the room, however, with his two *Self-Portraits* (as a young man and as an old man) and the interesting *Portrait of an Old Man* (1665).

The *Room of the Settecento* (Room 45), is the last in the Gallery. Reorganization lead to the creation of this heterogeneous collection of mainly Italian and French 18th-century works, which is also continued in the Vasari corridor. Canaletto (1697-1768) and Francesco Guardi (1712-1793) were both painters of Venetian scenes, and Pietro Longhi (1702-1785) and Rosalba Carriera (1675-1757) too were of the Venetian school. The French school is represented by the masterpieces of Jean Baptiste Chardin (1699-1779), Jean Etienne Liotard (1702-1789) and Jean Marc Nattier (1685-1766). The two splendid and elegant portraits by Francisco Goya (1746-1828) are recent acquisitions.

Our visit to the Gallery ends here. In the exit hall, designed by Buontalenti, is the marble statue of the *Wild Boar*, a Roman sculpture which was the model for Tacca's famous *Porcellino* fountain.

Canaletto, View of the Grand Canal.

Canaletto, View of the Doges' Palace, Venice.

PALAZZO
PITTI

The building of Palazzo Pitti was initiated by the rich, Florentine banker, Luca Pitti, when he was at the height of his political and economic power. Work on this enormous building at the foot of the Boboli hill in the Oltrarno area, was begun in 1458.

It is not clear who the original architect was, though the design has been attributed, without documentary evidence, to Brunelleschi (1377-1446). According to Vasari, however, the work of building was undertaken by Luca Fancelli. Brunelleschi's original plans consisted of the façade with three large doorways, alternating with four windows, which we see today. The two upper floors had seven full-length windows opening onto, and linked by, a narrow balcony.

Despite problems caused not only by the immense size of the building, but also by Pitti's political vicissitudes involving him in a conspiracy against Piero de' Medici in 1466, work continued on the building until his death in 1472. The building remained unfinished however, and in 1550 it was bought by Eleonora di Toledo, wife of Cosimo I, who also acquired the hill of Boboli behind, with the intention of creating a magnificent palace for the Medici court here. The task of enlarging and finishing the palace was thus given to Bartolomeo Ammannati (1511-1592), one of the most original artists in Florence during the second half of the 16th century. In the period from 1558-1570, he built the exquisite courtyard (one of the high points of 16th-century Florentine architecture) and added the two parallel wings of the building which run back in the direction of the garden.

These, like the 15th-century façade, are finished with huge blocks of roughly-hewn stone, known as Florentine rustication. A grotto was built at the end of the courtyard, containing the Fountain of Moses. The idea behind these additions was to create a building which, standing as it did on the edge of the city, would be a graceful combination of civic palace and country villa, looking out across the Boboli gardens, which were designed at the same time. In 1620 Cosimo II appointed the architect Giulio Parigi to continue the work.

The façade had already been altered by Ammannati who made the two lateral doorways into windows with low, bracketed sills, similar to those designed by Michelangelo, each decorated with a lion's head bearing the ducal crown. It was now extended, adding two rows of three windows, identical to the existing Brunelleschi ones, to each side, while on the ground floor Ammannati's design was repeated with three more low-silled windows. Under Ferdinando I, between 1640 and 1650, Parigi's son, Alfonso, completed the façade we see today. He extended the first and ground floors adding another five windows on each side, thus creating the two lowered wings, and lastly added another two windows with low sills to each wing.

The two rondò, which completed an already existing plan, were added at the time of the Lorraine. They were both built and completed in the early 19th century by Gaspare Maria Paoletti (1727-1813) and Pasquale Poccianti (1774-1858), who were also responsible for the *Palazzina Meridiana* in the south wing of the old palace. Towards the end of the Grand Dukes' reign (1850) Poccianti built not only the grand Neo-classical entrance and the monumental staircase leading to the upper floors in the east side of the building, but also the carriageway giving access to the Boboli gardens from Ammannati's courtyard. The large staircase leading to the Galleria Palatina was built in 1896 by Luigi del Moro (1845-1897).

In the course of time the interiors, as we can still see and admire, were decorated with stucco work and frescoes by the best artists and craftsmen of the day, and were sumptuously fitted out with furniture, fabrics and tapestries according to the tastes of the various princes and dukes.

Many artists worked on the building, including Bernardino Poccetti (1584-1612), who painted the frescoes in the Gallery and the *Sala di Bona*, in late Mannerist style; Volterrano (1611-1689); Giovanni da San Giovanni (1592-1663) who began the decoration of the large salon on the ground floor with the *Flight of the Muses from Parnasus to Florence* and the *Apotheosis of Lorenzo the Magnificent* at the time of Ferdinando II; Angelo Michele Colonna (1600-1687) and Agostino Mitelli (1609-1660), two painters from Bologna who frescoed the following three rooms with illusionistic architecture intended to soften their austere appearance. It was, however, Pietro Berrettini da Cortona (1596-1669), one of the greatest talents of the Baroque period, who was responsible for the most original and magnificent artistic project.

It was he who planned the rooms now housing the Galleria Palatina and once the ceremonial rooms of the grand-ducal appartment. These include the small *Sala della Stufa* on the first floor, rightly famous for its frescoed decorations, and the *Sale di Venere, Apollo, Marte, Giove* and *Saturno*,

View of the faéade.

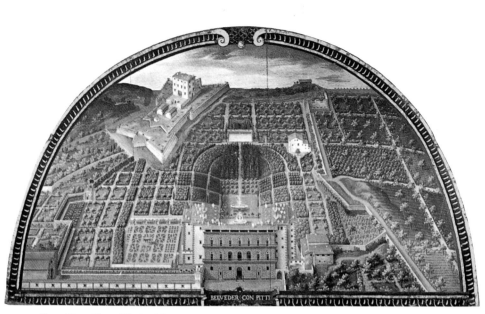

Giusto Utens, View of Pitti and the Boboli Gardens.

although this last has now been almost entirely attributed, at least for its execution, to a pupil of Piero's, Ciro Ferri.

Artists responsible for other rooms in the palace were Salvator Rosa (1615-1673); Antonio Domenico Gabbiani (1652-1727) a Florentine artist, and Sebastiano Ricci (1659-1734), a Venetian painter who had an important influence on the development of Florentine art later in the 18th century.

At the end of the 18th century, the resident Lorraine-Hapsburg family had a clear preference for the Neo-classical style and this lead to great changes in the decoration of many of the rooms. The Napoleonic period also brought with it many innovative elements, such as the two Empire style bathrooms called after the Grand Duchess Maria Luisa.

Under Ferdinando III and Leopoldo II, the rooms underwent further alterations, especially those used for official functions, now the State Appartments, where the original 17th-century style was completely eliminated. In 1828 Leopoldo II decided to open to the public several rooms containing works of art which had, until now, been part of an entirely private collection. Between 1865 and 1871, when Florence was the capital of Italy, the palace was the official residence of the king, Vittorio Emanuele II. Today Palazzo Pitti is rapidly becoming one of the most efficient and best-maintained museum complexes in Italy.

For many years now extensive restoration, alterations and re-organization have taken place, thus resolving some serious problems which affected the one-time residence, and enhancing both its artistic function and works.

One of the renovations carried out and well worth mentioning is the restoration of the twelve-roomed appartment on a mezzanine floor, between the first and second floors, known as the *Andito degli Angiolini*, made for Ferdinando de'Medici in the 17th century.

The palace today houses the Galleria Palatina, and the State Appartments as well as the Museo degli Argenti (silver and treasures), the Gallery of Modern Art, the Costume Museum, the Contini-Bonacossi Collection, the Porcelain Museum and the Carriage Museum.

GALLERIA PALATINA

The 16th-century staircase to the right under the portico of the palace courtyard leads up to the gallery. In the entrance, after the first room (the Anticamera degli Staffieri, or Footmen) some Roman and classical statues, brought here in the late 18th century, are exhibited. Here too are Caravaggio's *Toothpuller*, the *Triumph of Galateus* by Luca Giordano (1634-1705) and some examples of 17th- and 18th-century Dutch painting. This room was once the central part of the original loggia, from which the Grand Duke's family could watch plays and performances held in the palace courtyard and the amphitheatre of the Boboli garden.

One is immediately aware of a feeling of grandeur, quite different to that of the Uffizi. The rooms were sumptuously decorated with luxurious fabrics and boast magnificent frames, mainly dating from the time of the Medici who acquired the earliest works. These rare and beautiful paintings are intentionally arranged to resemble or re-create a typical 17th-century princely picture collection.

Since the paintings do not follow any chronological or thematic order, the effect is of an amazing host of masterpieces all together.

These are all part of the grand collection begun about 1620 by Cosimo II and later added to by his son Ferdinando II. Vittoria della Rovere later inherited many works from the Della Rovere family of Urbino, again increasing the collection. Cardinal Leopoldo, followed by Cosimo III, prince Ferdinando and Anna Maria Ludovica, and later again by the Lorraine family, all continued to add splendid works of art to the collection. It is recognized today that the gallery was created from both the Medici's private collection, as is traditionally accepted, but is also the result of a precise and positive cultural policy of the Lorraine family indicative of Florence's continuing humanist tradition.

Canova, the Venus Italica.

Some years ago, many other paintings, indicated by an asterisk beside the inventory number, were added to the Gallery's original collection.

These are mainly housed in the Volterrano Wing, previously part of the private royal appartments which, however, became part of the gallery in 1915, the year in which the reigning Savoy family donated the palace to the State.

Sala di Venere.

Titian, La Bella.

Our visit starts in the *Sala di Venere* which, at the time of Ferdinando II, was the entrance to the grand-ducal appartments. Richly decorated with allegorical scenes by Piero da Cortona (1596-1669), who also decorated the following four rooms, this room contains many important and interesting works of art. Four works by Titian, displayed here together, represent the general artistic development of that sublime genius of 16th-century Venetian art. His famous *Portrait of a Lady*, otherwise known as *La Bella* (1536) and painted for the Duke of Urbino, radiates the sophisticated and splendid beauty of this mysterious woman, so elegant in her jewels and fabulous dress.

This painting is notable particularly for its suberb execution, but also for the light touch and delicacy which Titian, influenced by new aesthetic ideas, abandoned shortly after. It would seem that this work is the first documented example of a portrait sold as a work of art, without therefore any reference to the subject. Attribution of the *Concert* has been a matter of uncertainty. It was bought by Cardinal Leopoldo as a work by Giorgione, but is now almost universally accepted to be by the young Titian, while still working in the master's circle.

It exudes a mood of anxious reflection in both the concept and the colour effect which is typical of Giorgione. In his later works, Titian transforms this into a warm, harmonious feeling for nature, both human and rural. Also highly perceptive are the *Portrait of Pietro Aretino* (1545), a famous intellectual and friend of many artists and patrons, and the *Portrait of Pope Julius II*, based on Raphael's painting of which there are many copies.

The *Seascape at Sunset* is by Salvator Rosa, a Neapolitan artist who worked at the Medici court between 1640 and 1649, mainly known as a painter of carefully observed landscapes, marine subjects, battles and allegorical scenes.

The *Peasants Returning from the Fields* is a landscape by Rubens who here succeeds in interpreting the wide open spaces in a truely Baroque manner, bathing them in the wonderful golden light of a sunset. *Ulysses in the Phaecian Island* is a companion piece to this landscape.

In the centre of this room is a magnificent sculpture, the renowned *Venus Italica*, one of Antonio Canova's (1757-1822) most beautiful pieces. The statue was commissioned in 1810 by Napoleon to replace the *Medici Venus* which, along with many other Florentine works of art, he had taken to Paris in 1779 from the Tribune in the Uffizi.

These were replaced however, in 1815. Although clearly classical in style, the sculpture is particularly beautiful for its grace and naturalness, and the delicate, almost realistic detail of the cloth Venus uses to try to hide her nudity, heavy with the water from which she is emerging.

The *Sala di Apollo* is richly decorated with frescoes, also designed

Titian, Mary Magadalen Penitant.

Titian, English Gentleman.

Salvator Rosa, Harbour at Dusk.

by Pietro da Cortona and painted by his pupil Ciro Ferri (1634-1689), representing the young Prince in conversation with Apollo.

The *Madonna Enthroned with Saints* (1522) was painted by Rosso Fiorentino for the Florentine church of Santo Spirito. The original painting was smaller than the one we see today, and was enlarged in the 17th century when it was added to the Pitti collection. Rosso Fiorentino, along with Pontormo, was one of the most original Florentine Mannerist painters and this splendid work demonstrates how new artistic ideas were moving away from the tranquil classicism of the early Renaissance towards a new-found sensitivity expressed here, however, with the kind of uncertainty which precedes the end of important historic and artistic periods.

Famous works by Titian here are the *Portrait of a Man* and the *Magdalen* (1531) in which a warm light pervades the colours, lending a golden glow to the hair and a pinkish tone to the skin.

Next is the small painting of *Federico of Urbino in the Crib* by A. Vitali, though once believed to be by Federico Barocci.

Andrea del Sarto, Medicean Holy Family.

Rubens, the Four Philosophers.

Titian, Portrait of Pietro Aretino.

The child's expressive face and the wealth of detail seen, for example, in the blanket and the embroidery on the cushion lend a particular charm to the painting. The range of colours used is carefully defined and limited. The *Portraits of Charles I of England and his Wife, Henrietta Maria of France* are by Van Dyke. Each is clearly described not only by aesthetic details but also by individual characteristics; the execution of the lace and the jewels which trim the clothes and armour, is particularly precise.

Two important paintings by Andrea del Sarto are the *Holy Family* and the *Medicean Holy Family*. The latter was painted for Ottaviano de' Medici during the last years of the painter's life and demonstrates all his compositional and chromatic ability.

The ceiling of the *Sala di Marte* was frescoed by Pietro da Cortona and portrays the *Triumph of the Medici Family* with their coat of arms in the centre. This room contains a splendid Baroque console table with a marble top and gilded and inlayed wood, with cherubs and lions holding a ball between their paws, a symbolic allusion to the city of Florence and the Medici.

Here too the quantity of paintings is almost confusing. Ruben's work, the *Consequences of War* (1638), dominates the room however.

This masterpiece was painted by the great Flemish artist in the last years of his life and both the allegorical purpose of the painting and the superb use of colour show Rubens at the height of his artistic ability: Venus tries to restrain Mars from going to war, the disasterous consequences of which are to be seen in the desperation of the figures and in the trampled paper and books, symbolic of culture, and the bold movement of the scene. Another beautiful work by Rubens is the *Portrait of Rubens, his Brother Filippo, Justus*

Rubens, the Consequences of War.

Anthony van Dyck, Portrait of Cardinal Bentivoglio.

Perugino, Madonna del Sacco.

School of Sustermans, Portrait of Galileo Galilei.

Raphael, La Velata.

Lipsius and Jan van Wouwer (the Four Philosophers) (1611-1612) which is in fact an early group portrait.

The details, such as the glimpse of landscape behind the red curtains, the tulips in a niche with a bust of Seneca and the two pens on the table, all combine to make the painting even more absorbing. Two paintings with the same subject here are by the Spanish artist from Seville, Murillo (1618-1682). Both these and his Madonna and Child represent the artist's desire to represent religious subjects with a lifelike softness and gentleness of expression and attitude, bathed in warm colours.

Lastly is Van Dyck's portrait of Cardinal Guido di Bentivoglio (c.1623), in his brilliant cardinal's red emphasizing not only his personality, as Rubens too would have done, but also his official capacity.

The Sala di Giove is also decorated with wonderful frescoes and stucco work designed by Pietro da Cortona. These represent the young prince, presented by Hercules and Victory, being welcomed to Olympus by Jupiter. This was once the throne room of the Grand Duke Ferdinando where he received official audiences.

The sculpture of Victory Seated is by Vincenzo Consani (1818-1887) and the tops of the beautiful Neo-classical, 18th-century tables are inlayed with semi-precious stones. The most famous work here is the Portrait of a Woman, also known as the Velata after the veil she wears, by Raphael. There is some doubt as to the identity of this serene and somewhat solemn young woman: some critics agree with Vasari, who states that the portrait is of Margherita, the daughter, also known as the 'Fornarina', of a Sienese baker, Francesco Luti, whom Raphael loved 'until his death'.

Others disagree with this suggestion however, claiming that some iconographic details, such as the veil which was used exclusively by married women at the time, excludes this possibility.

The fact that this beautiful woman is clothed in a sumptuous dress with richly embroidered sleeves, and is wearing jewellery, also clearly indicate that she was of aristocratic family. The painting has been cleaned, bringing to light the extremely delicate shading of white and grey, the mauve-grey background and the cold gleam of the skin tones.

Also in this room is a painting of *St. John the Baptist* by Andrea del Sarto, one of the most famous paintings of the saint as a young man. This painting demonstrates the artist's rigorous compositional ability, though his usual formal style is softened with a more gentle light. Highly delicate and sensitive is Perugino's painting of the *Madonna Adoring the Christ Child*, also known as the *Madonna del Sacco* after the bolster on which the child is seated, supported from behind by an angel.

The expressions of all the figures are touched with a gentle affec-

Raphael, Portrait of Agnolo and Maddalena Doni.

Raphael, the Madonna of the Grand Duke.

Raphael, the Madonna della Seggiola.

tion, including that of the young St. John, who stands with the Virgin in an elegant and radiant landscape. The painting of the *Holy Family* (1615) by Rubens is an example of this artist's originality and versatility.

He manages to temporarily ignore the weight of the many existing interpretations of this subject, portraying, with simplicity and tenderness, a family gathered around the crib of a newly born child.

We come next to the *Sala di Saturno*, frescoed by Ciro Ferri and dedicated to the god Saturn in allegorical glorification of the Medici family.

The room contains splendid works by Raphael from his Florentine and Roman periods. In his two portraits, *Maddalena Doni* (c.1505-06) and her husband *Agnolo Doni*, the sumptuous clothes and the rich jewels symbolically indicate the wealth of the couple portrayed, especially given that excessive luxury of dress was prohibited by law at the time.

The jewels in the necklace worn by Maddalena are highly symbolic: it is decorated with a unicorn, symbol of fertility; an emerald, signifying chastity; a ruby for strength and prosperity; a sapphire and a pearl to represent respectively purity and virginity. On the reverse of the panels are two episodes from the myth of Pyrrha and Deucalion by a later artist, auguring fertility.

Recent cleaning has restored the original beauty of the colour to this painting, removing heavy varnishes and 19th-century re-touching. X-rays have also revealed a change made by Raphael, who had initially portrayed Maddalena in a room with a window, similar to Flemish portrait painting. Next is the *Madonna and Child*, also known as the *Madonna of the Grand Duke* (1505-1506) as tradition relates that Ferdinando III was so fond of the painting that he kept it in his bedroom and even took it with him on his travels. This work too has been subject to restoration, revealing some interesting details one of which was also discovered by X-ray analysis. This showed, beneath the dark background on which the Virgin is placed, the interior of a room with a kind of window to the right, through which we can catch a glimpse of countryside.

The religious subject is here represented in a new style, inspired by

Raphael, La Gravida and detail.

Napoleon's Bathroom.

Leonardo, and already hints at the more complex, flowing, circular composition of the *Virgin and Child with St. John*, also known as *della Seggiola* (of the chair) (1514). This is one of the most famous, as well as most copied, of Raphael's works. The immense artistic ability and the original approach to colour which Raphael adopted are evident in this painting. The work also contains some symbolic details which have, in the past, given rise to various and unusual interpretations.

The seat, shawl and head covering of oriental design especially have been the cause of some strange theories. It was most widely believed that the model was a young woman of the lower classes with her two sons. In reality however, both the seat, which is similar to one reserved for high dignitaries at the papal court, and the shawl and head covering of oriental origin, costly accessories fashionable with aristocratic Italian ladies in the late 15th century, would seem to prove quite the opposite.

The *Portrait of Cardinal Inghirami* (1516) is nicknamed Phaedra after the dramatic role he played in Seneca's Hippolytus and is an exact and excellent study of the subject, a somewhat plump middle-aged man wearing his cardinal's gown. Here too restoration has revealed that the background painting conceals a curtain with delicate nuances of green. Two other works here, both by Perugino, are worthy of note: his *Mary Magdalen* (1476), once attributed to

Caravaggio, Sleeping Cupid.

Artemisia Gentileschi, Judith.

Leonardo, is sad and fragile, while the *Deposition* is a superb work, much enhanced by restoration which has emphasized the subtle artistic detail.

Next is the *Sala dell'Iliade*, completely altered during the Neo-classical period (1825-1829) and frescoed with scenes from the Iliad. In the centre is a statue of *Charity* by Lorenzo Bartolini (1777-1850). The room houses many works of considerable importance; the *Portrait of a Woman (La Gravida)* (1504-1508), by Raphael represents a pregnant woman, dressed plainly yet elegantly, and wearing, as was common in the 16th century, little but tasteful jewellery, notably a ring worn on the index finger.

The identity of the subject is unknown, though the small buffalos decorating the band around the hair net could perhaps be taken to symbolize the Bufalini family, from Città di Castello. It is, however, a masterful painting and cleaning has helped to emphasize the skillful placing of colour, the volumetric form and chiaroscuro effect of the figure, derived from Leonardo, but quite different to that of the *Portrait of Maddalena Doni*, already seen in the Sala di Saturno. The large painting of the *Assumption of the Madonna* or the

Panciatichi Madonna, (1526) is one of the best works by Andrea del Sarto. On the opposite wall, the *Passerini Altarpiece*, with its soft, bright colours, is a slightly earlier example, in which the celestial and terrestrial spheres are represented as being totally separate, a symbolism which was not at all traditional. Both works already anticipate the scenographic complexity of the Baroque period. In this room we finally come across the work of a woman painter, Artemisia Gentileschi (c.1597-1652), a noted and esteemed artist who worked mainly in Naples, here represented with *Judith* and *Mary Magdalen*.

Her work was influenced by Caravaggio's innovative example and with an elegant use of line and colour she created original optical effects, her figures, dressed in white and yellow for greater contrast, seeming to materialize from the shadows.

Many interesting works by Justus Sustermans (1597-1681), the Flemish portrait painter appointed to the court of the Medici in 1619, are displayed throughout the Gallery and in the State

Filippo Lippi, Madonna and Child.

Rachel Ruysch, Flowers and Fruit.

Salvator Rosa, Landscape with a Broken Bridge.

Appartments. Following the example of Velazquez, he painted his subjects with great precision, trying not only to capture personal characteristics but also to provide an accurate description of the details of their clothing.

In this room is his *Portrait of Waldemar Christian, Prince of Denmark*. A fine example of 17th-century, Spanish painting is *Philip IV on Horseback*, attributed to Velazquez, though more probably it was by a follower.

The *Sala dell'Educazione di Giove*, is named after the allegorical scene with Jupiter in the centre of the ceiling and, at the time of the Medici, this was the Grand Duke's bedroom. The *Sleeping Cupid* (1608) is a late work by Caravaggio, entirely encapsulating his artistic style, even in this small canvas. The skilful concentration of light on various parts of the body is used, for example, to give vigorous form to the mass.

The painting of *Judith with the Head of Holofernes* is, by contrast, a lavish work by Cristofano Allori (1535-1607), a Florentine painter whose range of colours and clarity of design seem inspired however, by the Venetian school.

To the right on leaving this room is the *Sala della Stufa* with frescoes representing the *Four Ages of Man* (1637), minor master-pieces by Pietro da Cortona.

Returning to the previous room and then proceeding, we come to Napoleon's *Sala del Bagno*, made for the Emporer's appartments in 1813. The rich, decorative plasterwork represents mythological scenes, while the statues in the niches represent the Nereids. The tables and stools furnishing the room are also in pure Neo-classical style.

The *Sala di Ulisse* follows. The ceiling was frescoed with the *Return of Ulysses* by Gaspare Martellini (1785-1827) and is a clear allusion to the return of Grand Duke Ferdinando III to Florence in 1815. There are works of various styles and schools here, including the *Madonna of the Impannata* (1513-1514) by Raphael, so called for the waxpaper-paned windows (impannate) in the background on the right.

This mature work of Raphael's represents the Virgin accepting the child from the arms of a more elderly figure, probably St. Anne, while another saint, perhaps St. Catherine, stands behind her. X-rays of the painting, taken when it was being cleaned, show two figures, one elderly and bearded, the other of a young man, in the place of the young St. John. The younger female saint also wore a veil.

The small painting by Filippino Lippi of the *Death of Lucrezia* was once part of a wedding chest in which newly weds kept their trous-seau. The artist's style here imitates that of Botticelli, who was a pupil of his father, Filippo. The scene in which the vivacious and colourful little figures are placed is defined by a rigorous and impec-cable perspective.

The *Sala di Prometeo* follows, with the myth of Prometheus

frescoed in the ceiling, the work of Giuseppe Collignon (1776-1863). With the exception of Raphael's *Madonna of the Seggiola*, already mentioned, all the 'tondi', those typically Florentine paintings, usually with a religious theme and intended for the private appartments, are collected together here. The outstanding work however, is Filippo Lippi's *Madonna and Child*, painted in the mid-15th century, possibly for the Bartolini family.

This is one of the most eloquent examples of the artist's creative spirit. The image of the Madonna and Child becomes a pretext for the detailed scenes painted behind the throne, depicting the Birth of Venus and the Meeting of Anne and Joseph at the golden gate, in a formal perspective.

They seem to be ordinary, everyday scenes, the figures moving lightly, as if in a dance, similar to those of his pupil, Botticelli, whose works are also in this room. Beneath the tondo by Jacopo del Sellaio (1442-1493) of the *Madonna Adoring the Christ Child*, is a work by Baldassare Peruzzi (1481-1536), *Apollo and the Muses*.

This same subject is repeated in the image decorating the surface of the marble table beneath. On the opposite wall are two portraits by Botticelli: *Portrait of a Woman*, frequently identified with Simonetta Vespucci, with whom Guiliano de' Medici was in love, though this attribution is uncertain, and the *Young Man Wearing a Mazzocchio*, a form of head-dress common in Florence in the 15th century.

Botticelli, Portrait of a Woman.

Next is a series of beautiful examples of the *Holy Family*, including one energetically executed by Luca Signorelli and one by Domenico Beccafume (1486-1551). A third, by Francesco Botticini (1446-1498), was previously attributed to Botticelli, but is in fact heavily influenced by contemporary Flemish painting which lead the artist to depict flowers, lizards and leaves in minute descriptive detail. Lastly is the extremely well-known *Young Bacchus* by Guido Reni (1575-1642), a painter inspired by the art of Annibale Carracci.

We return now to the *Corridoio delle Colonne*, named after the two columns of oriental alabaster on either side of one of the two doors. Paintings of the Dutch and Flemish 17th century are displayed here, including, on the left, a series of landscapes by Cornelis van Poelenburgh (1586-1667).

The following room, the *Sala della Giustizia*, takes its name from subject of the frescoes by Antonio Fedi (1771-1843) decorating the ceiling. The paintings are mainly Venetian 16th century and particularly important is the series of portraits by Tintoretto as well as Titian's *Salvatore* and *Tommaso Mosti*, and two *Portraits of Young Men*, one by Tintoretto and one by a follower of the Venetian school. The ceiling of the *Sala di Flora* was frescoed by Antonio Marini (1788-1861) and displayed here are later Mannerist Tuscan paintings by Andrea del Sarto, Alessandro Allori and Giorgio Vasari.

The next room, the *Sala dei Putti*, was also decorated by Antonio Marini and houses mainly still lifes, sea and landscapes and Flemish and Dutch paintings. Particularly ineresting is the painting of

Botticelli, Young Man wearing a Mazzocchio.

Flowers, Fruit and Insects (1716) by Rachel Ruysch (1664-1750). This is one of the best works by this female artist who preferred the still life genre, though at the time, in fact, it was also considered to be the only style which a woman ought to attempt. Ruysch succeeded however, in achieving an artistic ability of considerable charm.

Returning through the *Sala di Prometeo*, on the left we enter the small *Sala del Poccetti*, named after Bernardino Poccetti, previously believed to be responsible for the frescoes. They are now attributed to Filippo Tarchiani (1576-1645), a pupil of Matteo Rosselli (1578-1650). One is immediately drawn to the beautiful table (1716) made for Cosimo III and attributed to Giovan Battista Foggini.

The top is a mosaic of semi-precious stones, the legs are veneered with ebony and are heavily ornamented with gilded bronze and semi-precious stone decoration. On the walls are three lively paintings by Domenico Fetti (1589-1624): the *Lost Drachma*, the *Workers at the Vine* and *Saint Margaret of Cortona Defeating the Devil*. The *Portrait of a Man* is by Federico Barocci, the *Portrait of Francesco da Castiglione* by Pontormo, and the two *Portraits of the Duke and Duchess of Buckingham* are excellent works by Rubens.

Two other elegant rooms follow: the *Sala della Musica* and the *Sala del Castagnoli*.

The former, Neo-classical in style with columns at both ends, is light and spacious. The frescoes on the ceiling are by Luigi Ademollo (1764-1849) and represent the glorification of the Hapsburg family in the centre, and the liberation of Vienna from the Turks in the frieze. Under the beautiful chandelier is an ornate table with a top in Russian malachite (1819) by Philippe Thomire (1751-1843), while arranged around the walls are elegant, Neo-classical, drum-shaped tables.

The frescoes in the latter room were executed by Giuseppe Castagnoli (1754-1834), and in the centre is a magnificent table, one of the most famous pieces made by the Opificio delle Pietre Dure, dated early 19th-century. Designed by the Sienese sculptor, Giovanni Duprè (1817-1882), the top is inlayed with semi-precious stone and the feet are cast in bronze. Two large marble statues, copies of antique ones, representing a *Parthian Prisoner* and *Augustus Caesar*, are also exhibited here.

The next room is the *Sala delle Allegorie*, the first of a series frescoed by Volterrano (1611-1689). The scenes represent allegorical references to Vittoria della Rovere, wife of Ferdinando II, who lived in this wing of the palace. Some of the important works here are the *Rest on the Flight into Egypt*, by the school of Annibale Carracci, the *Portrait of a Woman* by the school of Bronzino, the *Virgin and Child with St. Catherine* by Giovanni da San Giovanni, the *Mary Magdelen* by Cigoli (1559-1613) and the *Trick of the Parish Priest, Arlotto* by Volterrano, a lively and imaginative portrayal of a priest, remembered for his love of jokes.

The ceiling of the *Sala delle Belle Arti* was frescoed with scenes representing the birth of the arts by Domenico Podestà (d.1862).

Displayed here are the *Apparition of the Virgin and Child to St. Francis* by Jacopo Ligozzi, the *Martyrdom of St. Steven*, and the *Madonna with Christ Child* by Cigoli, all of great expressive power. The *Sala dell'Arca* was frescoed by Luigi Ademollo in 1816 and the frieze represents David carrying the Ark of the Covenant in procession to Jerusalem. Housed here is an attractive late Roman marble bust of Jupiter. From this room one can also see the *Chapel of the Grand Duchess* which housed the religious relics belonging to the Grand Duke's family. The original late 16th-century altar was replaced during the last century by an altar panel by the Neapolitan painter Giovan Battista Caracciolo (c.1570-1637) representing the *Rest on the Flight into Egypt*. The Neo-classical furnishings are enhanced by vases from the Far East.

The short corridor on the right houses small 16th-century Dutch paintings, some Italian miniatures, works by artists from the court of Urbino and still lifes.

Volterrano, the Trick of the Parish Priest, Arlotto.

The *Sala di Ercole* was designed by the architect Giuseppe Cacialli (1770-1829), decorated by Pietro Benvenuti (1769-1844) and was named after the myths of Hercules which appear in the frescoes. In the centre is a large porcelain vase from Sevres with a gilded bronze setting (1784), while around the walls are attractive Neo-classical tables with fluted columns and porphry tops decorated with semi-precious stone mosaic, as well as 19th-century chairs.

The *Sala dell'Aurora* which follows is decorated with frescoes of Aurora and Pegasus by Gaspare Martellini (1785-1857); around them waft the allegorical figures of the arts and time. As well as paintings, here there are Neo-classical tables and a bust of Ferdinando III of Lorraine.

Two last rooms bring our visit to the Galleria Palatina to an end. The *Sala di Berenice* was frescoed with a scene of Titus Abandoning Berenice by one of the foremost Tuscan painters of the early 19th century, Giuseppe Bezzuoli (1784-1855). The walls are covered with a delicate 19th-century blue silk, and displayed here are mainly 17th-century Tuscan works, such as the *Martyrdom of St. Cecilia* by the Pisan painter Orazio Riminaldi. In the centre of the ceiling of the *Sala di Psyche* is the Rape of Psyche by Giuseppe Collignon (1776-1863). This room houses uniquely the paintings of Salvator Rosa, a Neapolitan painter who lived in Florence for nine years, leaving many examples of his work here. The *Landscape with a Broken Bridge* exemplifies his preference for paintings of ruins and his pre-Romantic style. Before arriving in the State Apparments we pass through the *Sala della Fama*, housing mainly minor Dutch and Flemish works, the vestibule and the bathroom of the Empress Maria Luisa, two most elegant Neo-classical rooms, furnished with Florentine furniture of the period.

THE STATE APARTMENTS

From the Palatine Gallery we now pass through the *Sala delle Nicchie*, arriving at the State, or ex-Royal, Appartments. These consist of a series of magnificent rooms where the Medici and Lorraine families once lived and which later belonged to the kings of Italy, passing from Vittorio Emanuele II to Umberto I and lastly Vittorio Emanuele III who donated the palace to the State.

Most of the decoration was carried out by artists during the Neo-classical period. The walls of many of the rooms are still decorated with fabrics from the time of the Lorraine.

The furnishings include beautiful tapestries and much of the furniture belonged to the Medici, Lorraine and later Savoy families.

The first room is the *Sala Verde*. On the walls are magnificent tapestries, woven in the Gobelins factory (1734-40), representing forty-nine *Stories of Esther*; the ceiling is decorated with early 19th-century monochrome frescoes by Giuseppe Castagnoli.

Of particular beauty is the ebony cabinet with mosaic panels of semi-precious stone, lapis-lazuli, bronze and carved and gilded wood, designed by Giovan Battista Foggini for the Grand Duchess, Vittoria della Rovere, wife of Ferdinando II.

The Queen's Bedroom.

The paintings here include Rubens' *Christ Arisen*, the *Allegory of Peace between Florence and Fiesole* by Luca Giordano and a picture entitled the *Study of Rubens* by an unknown Flemish artist.

We now come to the *Sala del Trono*, created when Vittorio Emanuele II of Savoy became king of Italy and Florence was proclaimed capital from 1865-1871.

The royal throne with its canopy is still in place.

The tapestries continue the *Stories of Esther* from the previous room, and the frescoes too are by the same hand as before. Above the door are the *Portrait of Henry IV of France* and a *Portrait of Maria de' Medici* by Sustermans (1597-1681).

Note also the French clocks and the antique vases from Japan and China.

The *Sala Celeste* is named after the beautiful blue material, dating from the time of the Lorraine, which covers the walls. The three tapestries, also Gobelins, were designed and made by Jans and Sonet (1690-1707), and the portraits of the Medici princes are by Sustermans.

The furniture is exquisite: the large console table, the chairs and stools are early 19th century; the smaller console tables, gilded, with a scagliola top, and the Sevres vases are, instead, 18th-century French and were brought from Parma.

Next is the *Chapel* with lavish Baroque decoration, partly re-decorated in the Neo-classical period when prince Ferdinando de' Medici's chamber was converted to become a chapel. After 1865 however, it was again altered, now becoming a drawing-room with the altar hidden behind a false wall. The *Madonna and Child* by Carlo Dolci (1616-1686) has an ornate frame in ebony decorated with jasper and tortoise-shell, gilded bronze and putti carved in semi-precious stone.

Also attractive are the two prie-dieu, one made of ebony and designed by Giovan Battista Foggini, and the other in ebony veneer, bronze and semi-precious stone, made in the Grand Duke's workshop.

The holy water stoup, shaped like a shell, has a dove in chalcedony, and the 17th-century cabinet is made of ebony and leather. The portraits on the walls are of the Medici, or members of the court and are by Sustermans, Gabbiani (1652-1726) and Cassana (1659-1714).

We are now in the *Sala dei Papagalli*, named after the wall covering, dating from the time of the Lorraine, which has a motif of a bird similar to a parrot.

This room, with a Neo-classical ceiling of gold and white stucco work, was once part of Queen Margherita's appartment.

The furnishings and accessories here too are all exquisite and among the portraits is a *Portrait* by Titian, traditionally thought to be of *Giulia Varano, Duchess of Urbino*.

Other portraits here are by Sustermans and Pourbus (1569-1622),

Pietro da Cortona and Ciro Ferri, The Sala di Apollo (detail).

Salotto di Cornelia, Meridiana Palace.

Detail of one of the rooms. while the still lifes are by Andrea Belvedere (c.1652-1732). Lastly, in a corner, is a large Austrian-style stove, decorated with stucco-work.

The *Sala Gialla* takes its name from the yellow brocade covering the walls. There are also four wonderful Gobelins tapestries (1735-45) portraying *Scenes of Louis XV Hunting.*

The beautiful Neo-classical chandelier came from Lucca and the *Portrait of the Palatine Electress* is attributed to J.F. Douven.

The *Queen's Bedroom* is next, with four more tapestries portraying *Louis XV Hunting.* The furniture is Empire style, mainly of Tuscan manufacture and probably made in Lucca for the Grand Duchess Elisa Baciocchi, the sister of Napoleon I.

The oval *Queen's Dressing Room* is a delightful room with elaborate plaster-work, partially coloured, and a lovely fireplace in mauve coloured marble. The silk covering the walls was specially embroidered with oriental motifs some decades later and the furniture is of a later period.

Returning through the *Sala dei Pappagalli* we come now to the *Apartment of Umberto I.* This group of four small rooms was specifically made to accommodate the King of Savoy and his wife while visiting Florence. The bedroom is decorated in white and gold and the furniture is mainly 19th-century. The rather beautiful French tapestry represents *Christ on the Cross. Umberto I's Study* is decorated with a silk wallcovering taken from a room in the villa of Poggio Imperiale and is also splendidly furnished.

The last two rooms are the *Salotto Rosso* and the *Salottino Giallo.* The latter is decorated with tapestries designed by Bronzino and made for the Apartments of Cosimo I in Palazzo Vecchio.

THE GALLERY
OF MODERN ART

Stefano Ussi, *Expulsion of the Duke of Athens.*

Silvestro Lega, *A Visit to the Studio.*

On the floor above the Galleria Palatina is the Gallery of Modern Art, founded in 1860 and subsequently re-organized and enlarged. Today it houses approximately two thousand works, mainly 19th- and 20th-century Tuscan art, but other Italian and foreign schools are also represented.

The gallery was renewed between 1972 and 1979, and the organization has remained largely unchanged since then.

The first nine rooms house works of the Neo-classical, Romantic and early 19th-century Purist periods. There are paintings by Pietro Benvenuti (1881-1859), Antonio Fontanesi (1818-1882), Francesco Hayez (1791-1882), Luigi Sabatelli (1772-1850) and sculptures by Antonio Canova (1757-1822), Lorenzo Bartolini (1777-1850) and Giovanni Duprè (1817-1882). In Room 10 are two wonderful bronzes of *Cain and Able* as well as portraits of famous men and historic scenes, themes continued in the next three rooms.

Room 14 houses the works of some Italian artists who were strongly influenced by the landscape school of Barbizon.

Room 15 is dedicated to the works of the Macchiaioli artist, Cristiano Banti (1824-1904). Banti's treatment of colour reminds us of Brett (1830-1902) melancholic Romanticism, while his technique is Pre-Raphaelite.

Giovanni Fattori, the Palmieri Rotonda.

Ottone Rosai, Tavern.

Frequently commissioned for genre paintings by the bourgeoisie, he managed to introduce scenes of country life into these works.

The portraits of Giovanni Boldini (1842-1931) who was a close friend of Banti, are, on the other hand sophisticated and stylish, achieving a level of elegance which is rather original.

The Martelli Collection in Room 16 contains paintings by the most famous Macchiaioli artists: Silvestro Lega (1826-1895), Telemaco Signorini (1835-1901), Federico Zandomeneghi (1841-1917) and Giovanni Fattori (1825-1908). These artists tried to renew the rather provincial style of painting common in Italy at the time by absorbing the innovative developments of French art.

The exhibits in Rooms 17-21 have patriotic, historic and contemporary themes, though the treatment is still extremely academic. The sculptures of Adriano Cecioni (1836-1886) alone express a more original and spontaneous, though at times almost grottesque, treatment of reality. In Room 20 is the *Expulsion of the Duke of Athens*, by Stefano Ussi (1822-1901). This was a significant work in the mid 19th-century representing a new 'Purist' style in the painting of classical history. Room 21 contains a large collection of portraits, some reflecting the new ideas from France, while others are still Romantic in style.

Rooms 24 to 27 house the most important examples of Macchiaioli painting, originally belonging to the collection of Leon Ambon, who donated them to the gallery. Fattori was fundamentally a realist painter and here we see many of his military, rural and marine scenes as well as the *Portrait of His Second Wife*. There are also similar works by Signorini and Lega.

'Macchiaioli' was the name first given to a group of artists who met at the Caffè Michelangelo in Florence between 1855 and 1867. Their intention was to create a non-academic style of painting, reproducing an 'impression of reality'.

The name was then applied to the typically Tuscan school which developed from it and which represented a very modern and revolutionary movement for 19th-century Italy. The intentions of these artists began to take form and the resulting paintings, almost always with natural and rural subjects, were painted using 'spots' (macchie) of colour and contrasting light. Traditional chiaroscuro was abandoned and dark and light colours were harmonized, thus obtaining an extremely luminous and highly atmospheric effect.

The innovations brought about by the Macchiaioli were not entirely formal however. Religious and historic themes were replaced by 'reality' which also occasionally included social reality. Of the Macchiaioli artists some of the most interesting were Giovanni Fattori, whose enormous opus included landscapes, Tuscan characters and military life, though not in formal, commemorative style; Silvestro Lega, who painted not only landscapes and portraits but also descriptive scenes of everyday life, and Telemaco Signorini who painted interiors and scenes representative of contemporary life.

Rooms 28 and 29, containing examples of central European art and of Italian decadentism, have a quite different atmosphere. Here the

Cristiano Banti, Secrets

Giuseppe De Nittis, In the Fields.

social theme is interpreted instead in the style of the Divisionists and the Symbolists.

Works such as those by Plinio Nomellini (1866-1943) demonstrate a dynamic expansion of colour which blurs form and outline.

The four small sculptures on pedestals are the work of the fine sculptor, Medardo Rosso (1858-1928). Here too the representation of reality and the positivist approach to a solid body is interpreted by a fusion of the form with the atmosphere, almost abolishing the outline. The periods of Post-Impressionism and Secessionist art are represented by the works of Giovanni Costetti (1874-1949) and Elisabeth Chaplin (1890-1982) in the last room.

ARGENTI MUSEUM

Pendants in baroque style with gold, pearls and precious gems.

It has already been mentioned that Palazzo Pitti also has an extremely beautiful collection of treasures and minor arts. Housed in a suite of magnificent rooms which were used as a summer appartment at the time of the Medici, later becoming reception rooms, the collection consists of fine cameos, inlayed stone-work, vases made of rock crystal and other semi-precious stones, statues in ivory, amber and coral, bronzes and ceramics, ornamental vases in various materials, and not only in silver as the name of the museum would seem to suggest. These pieces represent only part of the vast wealth and possessions of the Medici and Lorraine families, as well as various donations such as that of the Savoy family. Today these are all divided among the various Florentine museums.

The museum can therefore be considered as one of the most important collections of princely opulence in Italy. The entrance is on the northern side of the central courtyard and recently the collections have been reorganized. The first room was decorated in the 17th century by Giovanni da San Giovanni with allegorical scenes extolling the patronage of Lorenzo de' Medici. This was a waiting room for audiences, but it was also used for grand summer receptions when the doors on to the courtyard were opened. The steps under the windows are an architectural detail which was typical of Florence.

Continuing, on the right we come to the *Chapel*, decorated in the early 17th century, containing reliquaries, chalices and the *Capitular Cross* brought to Florence from the Salzburg treasury in 1815 by Grand Duke Ferdinando III.

The next room was frescoed between 1636-1641 by Michelangelo Colonna (1600-1687) and Agostino Mitelli (1609-1660). Among the exhibits here, for example, is a rare ebony cabinet with panels of semi-precious stone inlay and a lovely prie-dieu made in the grand-ducal workshops for Ferdinando II in the 17th century.

The next room, the *Private Reception Chamber*, is also decorated with frescoes by Colonna and Mitelli. Exhibited in the *Reception Room* are antique busts; 17th-century tables with mosaic inlay; an elaborate ebony coffer in Baroque style decorated with the Medici-Della Rovere coat of arms, and the *Stipo dell'Elettore*, a cabinet which was also made in the grand-ducal workshops to a design by Gian Battista Foggini. This was sent to Dusseldorf as a present from Grand Duke Cosimo III to his

daughter, Anna Maria Luisa, who brought it back to Florence in 1717.
The following rooms house an enormous range of objects which it would be
impossible to describe singly. We will therefore only mention those which
are the most important or best-known, the exquisite ivory vases, for
example, or the superb statue by the German Maestro delle Furie,
Curtius Leaps into the Abyss, in which the power and harmony of the
forces are perfectly emphasized by the subtle delicacy of the material
used. In the next cases are ivory sculptures with German and Flemish
scenes of martyrdom and crucifixion, as well as a series of reliquaries from
various countries and periods. Lastly, in front of the stairs leading to the
Treasury is a bronze *Crucifix* by the school of Giambologna. The Treasury
itself contains cameos, small vases and busts carved in semi-precious
stone, jewels, trays, plates, chalices, candlesticks and a pietradura mosaic
of Cosimo II in prayer, originally intended for the altar of San Carlo
Borromeo in Milan cathedral.
In the middle of a small room on the mezzanine floor is a beautiful Persian
carpet. Many unusual items are also displayed here ranging from ivories
and shells to coconuts, ostrich eggs and Bohemian crystal. Of particular
beauty however, is a silver travelling case made in Paris by master silver-
smiths for Ferdinando III. The following rooms contain a collection of
antique Chinese and Japanese porcelain. Returning to the lower floor we
reach the Bedroom of the Grand-Duke housing amber items mainly made
by 17th- and 18th-century German craftsmen. In the room beside is a
beautiful 16th-century table inlayed in semi-precious stone with the signs
of the zodiac, while the cabinets here contain various items in rock crystal.
Displayed in the cabinets in the last room of the museum, the *Sala Buia*
(*Dark Room*), are chalices, vases, and trays of Roman, Florentine and
Venetian manufacture as well as reliquaries. The Vase Collection of
Lorenzo de' Medici is of considerable importance. It consists of rare
Roman, Byzantine, Persian and Venetian examples, all bearing his name,
LAUR.MED., in Renaissance lettering. Many of these antique vases,
made from jasper, amethyst, chalcedony and sardonyx, were set in ornate
gold and silver mountings in the 15th century.

*Altar frontal with the Virgin
Enthroned.*

Baroque gold pendant.

*Caricature with baroque pearls
and enamelled gold.*

THE CONTINI-BONACOSSI
COLLECTION

Sassetta, Madonna of the Snow.

*Veronese, Giuseppe da Porto
With His Son, Adriano.*

The Contini-Bonacossi Collection, housed in eleven rooms, consists primarily of paintings, though sculptures, furniture and some minor arts are also represented.

The collection is of considerable artistic and historical value. It was donated to the state, which only agreed to accept it after twenty years of burocratic and legal disagreements, in 1974. Moreover, the number of works was reduced due to the decision of a committee which chose only works by those artists not already, or insufficiently, represented in the museums of Florence.

The collection contains Italian works of art by Duccio, Andrea del Castagno, Bellini, Tintoretto, Bramantino (c.1465-1530), Ferrari (c.1475-1546), Crespi (1665-1747), as well as highly important Spanish artists such as El Greco, Velazquez, Zubaran (1598-1664) and Goya. Two important sculptures are *Benedetto XIII* by Pietro Bracci (1700-1773) and *San Lorenzo*, an early work by Gian Lorenzo Bernini.

COSTUME GALLERY

The Costume Gallery was opened in 1983 and is evidence of the interest in, and new awareness of, the role of fashion. This has lead to the rediscovery and recovery of an almost entirely neglected branch of art and history. Thus today, after careful restoration, period clothing is exhibited for students, amateurs and enthusiasts alike to admire and study.

The Gallery has thirteen rooms, each dedicated to a specific period, recreating the evolution of dress from Napoleonic times to the early decades of the 20th century: from rigid corsets and voluminous crinolines, to short skirts revealing the legs.

Displayed here, therefore, are examples of the height of elegant dress in bygone days. The museum thus teaches us not only how we used to dress, but is also indicative of the cultural importance which many items, previously considered merely amusing, or strange, dusty mementos, have now assumed for us, whether a 17th-century lady's *habit à la française*, or a gentleman's embroidered tailcoat of the Napoleonic period. The items on display are changed every two years, and frequent temporary exhibitions are also held.

Three examples of walking dress.

CARRIAGE MUSEUM

Turning to the left as we come out of the doorway of Palazzo Pitti, is the entrance to the Carriage Museum. This houses a wonderful collection of berlins (a type of four-wheeled carriage), dating from the 16th to the 19th century. These belonged to the Duchess Maria Luisa of Tuscany, Duke Francesco II of Modena, Grand Duke Leopoldo II of Tuscany and King Ferdinando of Naples. The collection consists of seven carriages, two sedan chairs, a portable seat and various harnesses for an eight-horse coach.

Gala coach.

THE BOBOLI GARDENS

The Boboli Gardens take their name from the hill behind the palace and they extend from Palazzo Pitti to Forte Belvedere and across to Porta Romana. With a wealth of avenues, fountains, squares and statues, this is one of the most beautiful Italian gardens and today nature trails informing us of the plant and bird life, and piped classical music have made the park even more fascinating.
Eleonora di Toledo ordered the gardens to be made in 1550 and the

work was begun by Tribolo who died not long afterwards. The work *Neptune's Lake.* was then continued by Bernardo Buontalenti (1583) and was completed in the 17th century by various other architects, including Alfonso Parigi.
Although the entire garden is delightful, we will mention only some of the more important features.
One should first turn immediately to the left to visit the *Grotta del Buontalenti*, built by the highly imaginative creator of the park, a happy union of man-made structures and nature. Built between 1583

and 1590, it consists of three grottos. The first contains copies of Michelangelo's *Prisoners*; the ceiling was frescoed by Bernardino Poccetti and the walls are covered with stucco and petrified sponge forming strange landscapes and unusual figures. The second and third grottos, both frescoed by Poccetti, contain respectively, a sculpture of *Paris and Helen* by Vincenzo Rossi and *Venus* (1579-87) by Giambologna.

Returning on our steps, after the first square is the beginning of the large avenue with two marble Roman statues at the entrance. Continuing, we reach the first wide opening where we see not only the palace courtyard, but also the lovely *Carciofo* fountain (1639), by Pietro Tacca (1616/19-1686), which takes its name from the bronze artichoke on top.

View of the garden.

The 'Viottolone'.

We now come to the *Amphitheatre* with six tiers, a balustrade and niches which originally housed statues and vases. Building was begun

in 1599 and was probably finished by Alfonso Parigi in the 17th century. Spectacular theatre performances were held here in the past, often requiring complex scenery and stage sets. At the centre is a large antique basin in grey granite and an Egyptian obelisk.

The avenue leads to the *Lake of Neptune*, a large, shallow pond with a statue of Neptune by Stoldo Lorenzi (1565-68) as well as Naiads and Tritons. Nearby, to the left of the fountain is the *Kaffeehaus* (1776), a domed pavilion in Rococo style, designed by Zanobi del Rosso.

Continuing up the hill is the *Statue of Abundance*, begun by Giambologna and finished by Tacca. On the right are the *Garden and Palazzina del Cavaliere*, built in the ramparts of the walls which Michelangelo constructed for cardinal Leopoldo de' Medici in 1529. Enlarged at the time of Cosimo III, the palazzina was later altered by Zanobi del Rosso who made the double flight of steps. In the middle of the garden is the *Monkey Fountain*, possibly designed by Tacca.

PORCELAIN MUSEUM

The Porcelain Museum consists of three rooms inside the palazzina, housing choice examples of Italian, French, German and Viennese porcelain.

This is not an organized collection intended to illustrate the history of European porcelain, but was, instead, created for use by a court, with all its dynastic pretensions.

The museum was opened in 1973 and the first room is dedicated to Italian and French ware; the second to Viennese and the third to Meissen and Berlin.

Returning to the garden down a flight of steps, on the left we come to a wide, sloping avenue, known as the *Viottolone*. Lined by cypresses, pines and laurel bushes, it leads to one of the most elegant and attractive parts of the garden, a delightful combination of art and nature, the *Piazzale dell'Isolotto*. Designed by Alfonso Parigi (1680), the oval-shaped island is set in a large pool.

In the centre is a copy of Giambologna's *Oceanus*, the original of which is in the Bargello Museum. From here one can leave the garden through the Annalena gate, in Via Romana.

Service of Sevrès porcelain.

THE BARGELLO
MUSEUM

Previous page: Andrea della Robbia, Portrait of a Boy.

The Bargello, seen from the south.

This famous museum was created in 1859 by the provisional Tuscan government. It is situated in the *Palazzo del Podestà* or Bargello, one of the oldest public buildings in Florence, being some fifty years older than Palazzo Vecchio.

This imposing building around a beautiful crenellated tower known as the *Volognona* dates, in fact, from 1255 and was the official residence of the *Capitano del Popolo*. In 1261 it became the *Palazzo del Podestà* (town hall) and from 1502 it was also the headquarters of justice. Finally, in 1574, under the Medici, it became the residence of the chief of police (the 'bargello') and thus also the city's prison.

The original architect of this austere yet majestic building is unknown. It stands in the oldest part of the town, in Via del Proconsolo, and was built at the same time as the most important churches in Florence.

It could therefore have been the work of two Dominican monks, Fra Sisto and Fra Ristoro, with later additions by Neri di Fioravanti and Benci di Cione.

The building was later enhanced by elegant Gothic decoration such as double and single windows and battlements, and side and rear wings were also added, thus creating the elegant courtyard. The tower has been restored to its original beauty after three years of work and both it and the palazzo owe their present aspect to an extensive programme of renovation made necessary by various 19th-century alterations.

In the course of time the building had in fact been frequently disfigured, though the most extensive damage was caused when this beautiful public building was used as a penitentiary.

To adapt it to this purpose, many windows were closed up, the arches of the portico were filled in and the gallows were erected in the courtyard where the well now is.

Finally the palazzo, which had witnessed "bloody deeds and untold tragedy", became a National Museum and the room which once had been a torture chamber now houses works by Michelangelo, Sansovino (1486-1570) and Giambologna (1529-1608).

In the course of the last century therefore, the Bargello has become one of the most important museums of sculpture and minor arts in the world.

The works include statues, bronzes, majolica, amber and ivory pieces

previously in the Uffizi, weapons, coins and the seals of various public institutions, as well as more unusual items such as locks and keys from private collections. Some valuable donations are also housed here: the Carrand Collection of minor arts, left to the museum in 1888; the collection of weapons donated by Ressman in 1899 and the Franchetti collection of rare fabrics, 1906.

The ancient walls of the Bargello seem somehow to harmonize perfectly with all the items displayed here, whether weapons or majolica, bronze or ivory. Every single piece assumes a particular interest in this historic and atmospheric setting, complemented by the intelligent arrangement of the museum itself.

After the entrance and ticket hall, the first room we visit is that of *Michelangelo and 16th-century Florentine sculpture*, housing some of the most important Tuscan sculptures of that period, many of which were brought from the Uffizi. This is one of the oldest rooms in the building and has now been restored to its original beauty after the damage caused by the flood in November 1966.

At present the area towards the courtyard is entirely dedicated to the works of Michelangelo. The highlight of the room is his statue of *Bacchus* (1496-1497), one of the earliest statues made during the artist's Roman period and contemporary with his Pietà in San Pietro in Rome, it still reflects the influence of classical models. The half-open mouth and vacant eyes are a powerful expression of inebriation. Beside this is *Brutus* (1540) which Vasari maintained was an idealized portrait of Lorenzino de' Medici who killed Duke Alessandro de'

Anonymous, Courtyard of the Bargello.

Tuscan art, Female Figure.

Medici in 1537.

Although Michelangelo was inspired by the busts of classical antiquity, he demonstrates here an original and intense quality, emphasized by the juxtaposition of the body with the head, in sharp profile. Opposite is the *Pitti Tondo* (1504-1508) which reveals instead the influence of Leonardo and is reminiscent of the slightly earlier *Doni Tondo* in the Uffizi.

Here too the three powerful and vigorous figures are enclosed within the limits of a circle from which they try, delicately and rythmically, to break free. The face of Mary anticipates those of the Sybils which Michelangelo was to paint later in the Sistine Chapel in the Vatican.

Separated by a curved, plastic structure is the rough-hewn statue of *David-Apollo* by Michelangelo, dated 1530-32 like the statues for the New Sacristry in the Medici Chapels.

Other notable works here are the *Tondo* by Giovan Francesco Rustici (1474-1554); the *Bacchus* by Jacopo Sansovino; the *Bust* of Cosimo I, a splendid work by Benvenuto Cellini (1500-1571), as too are his other bronzes of *Perseus, Mercury, Danae, Minerva* and *Jupiter*, the relief panel of *Perseus Liberating Andromeda* and the marble *Narcissus*. Lastly are two works by Giambologna: the *Victory of Florence over Pisa* (1570), a marble statue previously in the *Salone dei Cinquecento* in Palazzo Vecchio, and the bronze *Mercury* (1564) whose taut body, rising from the first toe of his left foot to the index finger of his right hand is a quite masterly achievement.

Small display cases contain preparatory drawings by various 16th-century Florentine artists.

We now come to the elegant 13th-century courtyard with, on three sides, a portico of rounded arches on octagonal columns and cross vaults. On the fourth side is a stairway made by Neri da Fioravanti between 1345 and 1367.

This brings us up to the loggia with double arches and octagonal pilasters, built in 1319 by Tone di Giovanni. On the second floor are Gothic triple windows.

In the centre of the courtyard is a well and on the walls under the portico are the coats of arms of the councillors and magistrates who held office from the 14th to the 16th century, as well as the emblems of the city's quarters and districts in polychrome relief.

Under the spacious portico are various sculptures. Starting at the exit from the first room and working in anti-clockwise direction are two 14th-century stone lions with iron crowns bearing lilies, which came from Piazza della Signoria; a statue of *Clio* by Poggini; the *Canon of St. Paul*, made in 1638 and brought from Livorno; *Oceanus* by Giambologna and *St. John the Baptist*, recently attributed to Gian Lorenzo Bernini. Also interesting are the 16th-century *Lamp-lighter* by Giulio Serafini, previously in Palazzo Gualtiero in Orvieto, and the statue of *Cosimo I de' Medici* in Roman dress, by Vincenzo Danti (1530-1576), previously in the Salone dei Cinquecento in Palazzo Vecchio. The portico opposite the stairs houses statues by Bartolomeo

Tino da Camaino, Madonna and Child.

Michelangelo, Brutus.

Ammannati.

Michelangelo, Pitti Tondo.

We come next to a room of *14th-century sculptures* containing medieval pieces taken mainly from Florentine buildings when being demolished or altered. The 14th-century stone aedicule, situated by the door, came from the church of Santa Maria Novella as did the 13th-century column in the middle of the room, with the sculptures of *Sts. Peter and Paul with Two Monks*. Corresponding to this on the left are three *Acolytes* by Arnolfo di Cambio (c.1245-1302), previously in the Ark of the Covenant in San Domenico, Bologna. Displayed on a corner shelf are four small stone statues of the *Prophets*, taken from the church of Orsanmichele.

At the far end of the room, on a base which emphasizes its vast size, is a *Virgin with Sts. Peter and Paul* by Paolo di Giovanni (active 1322-45), taken from the city gate of Porta Romana. Although much eroded,

Sansovino, Bacchus.

the form and expressive quality of the figures are still quite clear.

We come finally to the most important piece in the room, the fine, marble *Madonna and Child*, attributed to Tino da Camaino (1285-1337). Almost opposite this, on the right-hand wall is the allegorical *Caryatid* by the same artist.

We reach the first floor by the internal staircase. On the walls are oval portraits of members of the Medici family (1560-1574) by Francesco Ferrucci del Tadda (1497-1585).

At the end of the corridor with sculptures of birds by Giambologna, is the *Sala degli Avori*, containing mainly items from the Carrand Collection.

This provides a fascinating account of the history of ivory sculpture from the 5th to the 17th century. At present these are complemented by items in different materials such as wood, leather and bone. The ivories are of Greek-Byzantine, Mesopotamian, Indian, Arabian, ancient Sicilian, Moorish, and northern European origin and consist of holy diptychs, caskets, ciboriums, crucifixes, knife handles, combs, small statues and hunting horns. It would be impossible to list and describe the delicate beauty of them all. In the first display case, however, is a *Madonna and Child* which, given the deep hollow behind the seat, was probably intended to be a reliquary. There are also an attractive *Crucifix* (c.1190) from the Ile de France, and some delicately carved, 13th-century mirror-backs, which medieval ladies used to carry on belts at their waists.

There is also a wonderful *Chessboard*, with the game of backgammon on one side, decorated with borders containing hunting and battle scenes and musical concerts, similar to those seen in French miniatures of the period. Immediately to the right of the entrance is a 14th-century wooden sculpture of a *Bishop Saint*. Once painted and gilded, it had suffered considerable damage but has now been completely restored to its orignal state. The panel paintings and decorated wooden statue on the walls are all of various origins. The *Bust of St. Peter* by Domenico or David del Ghirlandaio is a rare 15th- or 16th-century museum piece.

We now come to the *Chapel of Mary Magdalen*, decorated with a cycle of frescoes representing *Paradise and Hell* by the school of Giotto, including a *Portrait of Dante* and *Scenes from the life of Saint Mary the Egyptian* and *Mary Magdalen*. The chapel is furnished with late 15th-century wooden stalls and a lectern taken from the monastery of San Bartolomeo at Monteoliveto, made, however, for San Miniato al Monte. The display cases contain mainly ecclesiastical items in gold, as well as a 15th-century triptych of the *Madonna and Child with Saints* attributed to Giovanni di Francesco.

The room preceding the chapel is now called the *Sala Carrand* although it was previously known as the *Sala del duca d'Athene*, and here too most of the works are from the Carrand Collection. Again, we can only mention the most representative items.

In the area closest to the chapel are two display cases with antique and modern jewellery. In the first are beautiful French, Lombard,

Byzantine and Renaissance items, including hair-clips, brooches, earrings, bracelets, mosaics and cameos. In the second are fine examples of jewellery from the 15th to the 18th century, including unusual rings with settings in the form of leaves, hands or paws, mainly of the latter period.

Opposite are two cases containing enamels, Renaissance painting and some Limoges items, including a particularly beautiful plaque of the *Virgin Seated with Child*, taken from a print by Marcantonio Raimondi (c.1482-c.1534). There is also a large oval plaque with a *Portrait of a Prelate* by Leonard Limosin (c.1505-1575/77), and twelve smaller plaques for a chest, with cupids on a red background.

Around the walls are exquisite little paintings from the 14th to the 16th century, of which the most important are the famous *Carrand Diptych*, a late 14th-century French painting, and, opposite, a *Noli Me Tangere* and *Coronation of the Virgin*, by the Master of the St. George Codex (early 14th-century), a pupil of Simone Martini.

Near to the fireplace, opposite the window is a case containing an interesting collection of variously-shaped buckles, while the case beside has examples of Indian art.

The first case in the centre has some examples of Wunderkammer, with an especially beautiful 16th-century French casket made of gilded and enamelled bronze. Also in the centre of the room are panel

Michelangelo, Bacchus.

Cellini, Bust of Cosimo de' Medici.

Bartolomeo Ammannati, Leda.

Imperial Byzantine Diptych.

paintings of the *Annunciation* and the *Presentation at the Temple*, as well as two more cases containing medieval, ecclesiastical items in gold.

One of the most lovely of these many, important items is the *Altar Cross* in gilded and enamelled silver, clearly by an important French artist of the 14th century.

In the penultimate case are scientific instruments and clock and watch mechanisms, while the last case contains oriental items, announcing the theme of the next room. The last display cabinet on the right contains the oldest items of jewellery and enamel in the collection.

The 12th-century *Pastoral Scene* from the area of Lorraine and the similar piece from Limoges, decorated with fanciful flowers and enamel arabesques, are of especial beauty.

The *Sala Islamica* contains Islamic works of art from the Carrand, Franchetti, Ressman and Grand Dukes' collections. In the first case in the centre and in the one beside it, are metal items, such as the two lovely scent bottles from Syria (14th and 15th centuries), and a splendid bowl with astral decorations in gold and silver. The third cabinet contains coins, enamelled tiles, a rare necklace, Venetian-Saracen items and a lamp, decorated with enamelled glass, from a Mosque. Displayed on its own in one case is a beautiful jug, dated between 1363 and 1377, while other cases house ivories, glass, Persian and Turkish tiles, fabrics, carpets, jewellery and lastly weapons from the Grand Dukes' collection.

We now come to one of the most beautiful, and certainly the most important room in the palace. Originally the Council Chamber, it is now the *Sala di Donatello* housing 15th-century sculptures. First are the famous *Panels* by Ghiberti (1378-1455) and Brunelleschi, made for

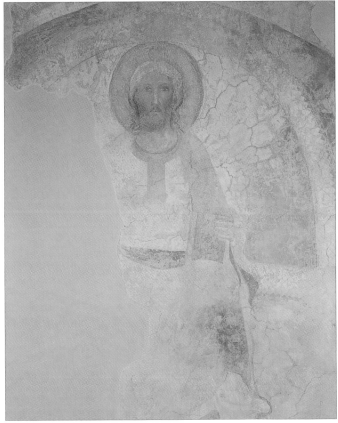

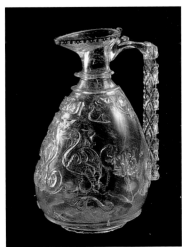

School of Giotto, fresco from the Chapel of St. Mary Magdalen (detail).

Jug in rock crystal and reliquary cross.

the renowned competition of 1401 for the North door of the Florentine Baptistery. Next is a series of *Madonnas* by Michelozzo (1396-1472), Agostino di Duccio (1418-c.1481) and Luca della Robbia (c.1400-1482), a young *St. John*, a bust of a *Girl* and of a *Young Woman*, two exquisite and delicate marble sculptures by Desiderio da Settignano (c.1430-1464).

We should look at Donatello's works in chronological order, rather than follow their physical arrangement. First is the marble *David*, made about 1408 when Donatello was working on a series of marble sculptures for the cathedral.

The statue was, in fact, intended for the the lower part of a spur in one of the tribunes of the apse, which then became the base of the dome. It may however, have been too small for the space it should have occupied, for in 1416 it was given to the Signoria, who placed it in the Oriolo Room in Palazzo Vecchio. We come next to *St. George*; while Donatello continued to work for the cathedral, he also completed other great masterpieces, including this, made for Orsanmichele between 1416-1419.

The suggestion of movement is a constant element in Donatello's work and here it has become the principle feature of the statue. There is the slightest suggestion of a gesture which is so vivid and energetic however, that its intense dramatic effect is similar to that of a

Mameluk jug in engraved, beaten copper.

Donatello, St. George.

Bronze horseman.

Donatello, Cupid.

painting. The same intensity is seen in the bas-relief on the base of the statue representing *St. George and the Princess*.

In the centre of the room is a pietra serena sculpture of the *Marzocco* (1420), a lion and one of the symbols of Florence, holding the arms of the city. Originally destined for the Papal Appartment in Santa Maria Novella, it was placed outside Palazzo Vecchio in 1812. The crisp, incisive style perhaps derives from the sculptural tradition of Nicola Pisano. Alongside is the bronze *David* made in 1430 for Cosimo I.

Of all the many figurative representations of this popular biblical hero, this is without doubt closest to the Old Testament description of "young, handsome and fair", clearly an adolescent. David is, in fact, portrayed immediately after the act of killing Goliath, very young, with his face slightly in shadow, making him seem even more mysterious and intense, while the light falls fluidly over the rest of his body.

Lastly is the sculpture of *Amore*, (1430-40) for a long time believed to be Etruscan. At the beginning of the 16th century it was in the possession of the rich merchant, Agnolo Doni, a collector and friend of Raphael, and in 1778 it was given to the museum.

We now come to the elegant loggia known as the *Verone*, with various 16th-century sculptures.

The bronze figures of animals, such as the *Turkey from the New World*, *Eagle*, *Owl* and *Barn Owl* came from the Tribolo Grotto at the Medici villa at Castello.

The next room houses the Bruzzichelli donation, given to the Museum in 1983 by a well-known Florentine antiquarian. The collection

Donatello, Bust of Niccolò da Uzzano.

Donatello, David.

Brunelleschi and Ghiberti, panels with the Sacrifice of Isaac.

Andrea Verrocchio, Woman with Flowers.

Desiderio da Settignano, Young Woman.

Donatello, St. John the Baptist.

includes a ciborium, tabernacle, table, chairs and sideboard as well as bas-relief panels and mosaics. *The Madonna and Child* by Jacopo Sansovino is a particularly expressive piece.

The last room on the first floor is the *Sala delle Maioliche*, where the entire collection of splendid maiolica has recently been arranged. Beginning on the left, the order of arrangement is historical and geographical, with examples of antique ceramics, such as the *Rinfrescatoio* (14th-15th century), as well as pieces from Faenza, Deruta, Casteldurante, Gubbio and Venice.

Most of the pieces, however, are from both Urbino, such as the beautiful circular bowls and the large elliptical plates, and from Florence. Among the many pieces of Medicean porcelain, for example, are an attractive medallion with the bust of Francesco I; three pharmacy jars, previously in the monastery of San Marco, and an enormous 17th-century jar for vin santo. Of a later date, however, are the pieces from Savona, Angarano, Milan and Faenza, displayed beside 19th- and 20th-century Tuscan porcelain from the Cantagalli, Signa and Doccia factories.

In the last cases are 15th- and 16th-century Spanish and Moorish pieces. Finally are the large, glazed terracotta pieces by Giovanni della Robbia (1469-1529), *St. Francis* and *St. Ursula*, displayed above the cases.

On reaching the second floor, we come to the *Sala di Giovanni della Robbia*, son of Andrea and great-nephew of Luca. The works here are from the final period of the Della Robbia workshop. To the left of the stairs is the *Presepe*, one of Giovanni della Robbia's early works, while the *Pietà* is a later piece.

The two large lunettes are from the convent of Santissima Annunziata. The *Bacchus* belonged to the Medici and is one of the artist's rare non-religious works. Although many of the other pieces here are by unknown artists, they are still of considerable beauty. The cases contain plaques of various periods and origin.

The next room contains sculptures of the late 15th century, mainly brought from the Uffizi.

The delicate *Bust of a Woman* is by Verrocchio (1435-1488); the bust of *Machiavelli* is attributed to Antonio del Pollaiolo; the historian *Matteo Palmieri* is by Rossellino (1409-1469) and lastly, Verrocchio's *David* was made in 1476 for the Medici villa at Careggi and was later placed in the entrance to the Sala dei Gigli in Palazzo Vecchio.

The two figures of the *Madonna* are also by Verrocchio, while the fine angular bust of *Battista Sforza*, which came to Florence as part of the Della Rovere inheritance, is by Francesco Laurana (1430-c.1502). A recently discovered and restored *Crucifix*, attributed to Verrocchio, was added to the exhibits in this room in December 1994. Though Vasari mentions others, this is believed to be the only remaining wooden crucifix made by the artist.

The *Sala dei Bronzetti* contains many small bronzes, some from the Uffizi, others from Palazzo Pitti, the villa of Poggio Imperiale, Palazzo Vecchio and the Carrand Collection.

Andrea Verrocchio, David.

M. Soldani Bensi, Dancing Faun with Cymbals.

The great number of items displayed is indicative of the interest collectors had in these items in the 16th century. They have recently been arranged according to style and period.

The first case on the left contains items with a classical theme, such as the various examples of the *Laocoon* or the copy of the equestrian statue of *Marcus Aurelius*. Almost all the small bronzes in the second case are copied from Michelangelo, such as the *Bacchus*. Next are bronzes by Andrea Riccio (1470-1532) from Padua and, on the opposite

Helmet with Eagle's Head.

wall, bronzes by Baccio Bandinelli (1488-1560).

The first two display cases in the centre of the room contain works by Giambologna and his school. The works in the case against the wall are exclusively by Giambologna, however, such as several small *Venuses*, the *Musician* and two terracotta heads.

Other works worthy of note here are the *Dwarf Morgante on a Dragon*, by Giambologna and Vincenzo della Nera and the elegant *Greyhound* by Benvenuto Cellini.

Later works are the *Killing of Argus* by Foggini and *Hercules and Antaeus*, a work renowned for its supreme skill, made by Antonio Pollaiolo for Guiliano de' Medici. Most unusual are the bronze items made for everyday use, such as little bells, mortars, lamps, candlesticks and figures of animals.

We now come to the last rooms of the museum. The *Sala di Andrea della Robbia*, previously known as the Cellini Room, has glazed terracottas by Andrea, nephew of Luca della Robbia. Of note here are the delicate *Portrait of an Unknown Man*, the touching bust of a *Young Boy*, (c.1470) and the larger work, *Madonna of the Architects*. Between the two windows is a lovely stone basin (1499), originally in Palazzo Acciaioli in Via Santissimi Apostoli.

The *Sala degli Armi* houses weapons from the Medici, Carrand and Ressman collections. Some famous items from the medieval period are the pair of gauntlets, dated 1374 and a beautiful hunting horn, which probably belonged to Lorenzo the Magnificent.

In the cases are Medicean lances and ceremonial arms which belonged to the Dukes of Urbino, the Della Rovere.

Particularly interesting are the suit of armour and a visored helmet, used by soldiers in feudal times, made by Filippo (active 1532-45) and Giovanni Negroli (active 1525-1565) for Guidobaldo II della Rovere.

There are also many other 17th-century long and short arms; 18th- and 19th- century hunting arms; part of a horse's armoury, which belonged to Francesco Maria II, Duke of Urbino, and the ceremonial armour of Grand Duke Ferdinando I.

This art gallery was founded in 1784, by Grand Duke Pietro Leopoldo of Lorraine, when he decided to donate a collection of classical works of art to the Accademia di Belle Arti for use and study by the students. At the time, the processs of copying great artistic works of the past was still considered to be fundamental to learning drawing skills.

The collection was, and still is, in the prestigious complex of buildings which houses the important institutions of the school of art, the music school, now known as the Luigi Cherubini Conservatory, and the Opificio delle Pietre Dure.

Two buildings were altered and adapted to house the collection: the Ospedale di San Matteo, and the convent of the nuns of San Niccolò di Cafaggio. The two courtyards of the Scalzo and of the Voti della Santissima Annunziata were also absorbed into the Accademia.

The items were mainly taken from the Medici collections but later these were considerably enriched by works taken from the religious orders suppressed in 1786 and in 1808-10.

It was therefore re-organized in 1841 and the exhibits were arranged chronologically. In 1859 the collection of the Galleria d'Arte Moderna was added to the museum, though it was entirely transferred to Palazzo Pitti in 1913. The present entrance was opened in 1882 and some rooms belonging to the Opificio delle Pietre Dure were added.

The Tribune, designed by the architect De Fabris (1808-1883) for Michelangelo's David, was also made at this time, and ever since then the famous sculpture has been the symbol of the gallery itself. The statue was brought here in 1873 from its previous position outside Palazzo Vecchio and a model of the original wooden cart used to transport it is exhibited to the left.

Works of art were frequently exchanged between the Gallery and the Uffizi, but the most recent programmes of reorganization took place in the 1950's, again in 1976, when the Colossus room was altered, and more work was recently completed in 1985.

The new rooms on the first floor, which had never previously been used, contain Florentine paintings of the late 14th to the mid-15th century.

Recently opened on the ground floor is the Salone delle Toscane, dedicated to early 19th-century Tuscan art. Displayed here in their entirety for the first time, are Lorenzo Bartolini's original plaster cast models. A professor at the Academy he was, together with Canova, Thornvaldensen (1770-1844) and Luigi Pampaloni (1791-1847), one of the most important 19th-century European sculptors.

Page 9?: Michelangelo, David (detail).

Filippino Lippi, St. John the Baptist and St. Mary Magdalen.

The entrance hall was frescoed by Giuseppe Maria Terreni (1739-1811) and houses a Neo-classical marble statue of *Diana* by Gaetano Grazzini (1786-1858). The ticket office is now in the *Sala dell'Anticolosso*, and from this we reach the *Sala del Colosso* where an important selection of early 16th-century Florentine art is housed. On both sides of the entrance are panels portraying *Job* and *Isaiah*, by Fra' Bartolomeo della Porta (1475-1517). On the right are two pieces by Francesco Granacci (1469-1543), an early 16th-century artist who was an apprentice in Ghirlandaio's workshop together with Michelangelo, three years his junior. Still on the right are two tondos: a rather lovely *Holy Family* by Franciabigio (1494-1524) and a *Madonna and Child with St. John* by Girolamo del Pacchia (1477-1535). These artists were part of that extensive group of minor masters who were not involved with the problems of artistic innovation, yet constituted the main body of professional Florentine artists. More than the great masters, they were in contact with their aristocratic clients and interpreted the compositional and stylistic developments initiated by Raphael, Michelangelo and Leonardo, in a more simple and comprehensible manner.

Next are two panels representing *St. John the Baptist* and *Mary Magdalen* by Filippino Lippi, both from the church of San Procolo in Florence. The two figures are portrayed in deeply shadowed niches, which emphasize the feeling of sorrow and anguish, visible in their pose and the somewhat brisk and introspective use of colour. The *Deposition* in the centre of the wall is of considerable interest. Begun by Filippino Lippi, it was intended for the main altar of the Santissima Annunziata church in Florence, but it was completed by Perugino, who also reworked the upper part. The stylistic difference is obvious if one considers the degree of control in the painting. The dramatic episode is portrayed both by Perugino's formal purity and by Filippino's tragic and disturbing vortex of figures, colours and space.

After the *Virgin and Child with Saints* by Ridolfo del Ghirlandaio (1483-1561) is the majestic panel of the *Virgin Enthroned with Saints and Angels*, also known as the *Pitti Altarpiece* by Fra Bartolomeo. Painted in 1512 for the church of San Marco, it shows the mystic marriage of Saint Catherine with the Christ child placing the ring on her finger. Among the saints, on the right is Saint Bartholomew, which clearly inspired Andrea del Sarto's Saint John the Baptist painted in 1517 for the famous *Madonna of the Harpies* panel. Note also the strongly geometrical structure of the

composition, with its circular movement of form, culminating in the conical shape of the cloth held by a flight of angels. This is one of the most important European works of art of this period.

The centre of the room is dominated by Giambologna's plaster-cast model for the marble group of the *Rape of the Sabine Women* (1582), destined for the Loggia dei Lanzi. Modelled on Michelangelo's works, the twisting structure of this vigorous group is pervaded by the dynamic clash between forces, achieving a supreme virtuosity which makes it one of the best examples of Mannerist sculpture.

The seven magnificent tapestries from Brussels usually displayed in the *Grand Salone*, are at present being cleaned and restored.

The corridor and Tribune are dedicated to the works of Michelangelo Buonarroti.

Displayed here are the *David*, which c immediately, and four of the *Prisoners* (or S tomb of Pope Giulio II in San Pietro in Michelangelo's death, however, they were Cosimo I, who had them placed in Buontalen Gardens. In 1909 they were replaced by co were brought to the museum.

Perugino and Filippino Lippi, Deposition with detail on the following page.

Maestro della Maddalena, Mary Magdalen Penitant (detail).

These four pieces were probably begun betw the left is the *Awakening Slave* and the *Atla* is *St. Matthew*, the *Young Slave* and the *Bea* zing unfinished style of the Prisoners, froz which enclose them, was Michelangelo's i expression. It was not a fortuitous discovery suggesting, perhaps, a new stylistic development. Emerging from these roughed-out masses is the sensation of forceful vitality, attempting to liberate itself from the material which still weighs it down.

The statues are striking for their dramatic agitation, the interior torment, their closed and anguished expressions, struggling without any hope of success against the spiritual bonds symbolized by the marble which itself conceals unknown, internal elements.

Of the twelve Apostles commissioned from Michelangelo by the Woolmakers Guild and the cathedral workshop for the chancel of Florence cathedral, the statue of *St. Matthew*, also unfinished, is the only one to have been begun. It was brought to the Accademia from the Opera del Duomo in 1834. In this lovely work the saint seems to be using an immense effort to try to liberate himself from the material which forms him, thus emphasizing the dramatic conflict between body and spirit.

After the *Bearded Slave*, is the *Palestrina Pietà*. This belonged to the Barberini family and it was brought to the gallery in 1940 from the church of Santa Rosalia in Rome. This is the only work whose attribution to Michelangelo is uncertain.

On the back one can still see traces of the sketch of a Roman ruin, used by the artist in the painting. Although the date of 1550 is generally accepted, critics are not unanimous about its attribution. It is, however, a highly dramatic work: the weight of Christ's

smooth body, vibrant with light, is supported by the sketchy but fluid forms of the Virgin and Mary Magdalen.

We now come to the *David* (1502-04), the most famous sculpture in the history of Italian art, proudly occupying the entire circular area of the Tribune. Vasari said of the work, "To be sure, anyone who has seen Michelangelo's David has no need to see anything else by any other sculptor, living or dead."

The statue is best studied following an ascending, anti-clockwise direction; the axis of the figure falls from the head to the right foot, in a series of brisk bounds which are not dispersed, but remain instead concentrated in the body and its desire to act. Michelangelo did not portray David in the act described in the Bible, but in the moment of tension before, concentrating not on the action, but on the intention.

The sculpture was made from a tall, narrow block of marble which Agostino di Duccio, a Florentine sculptor, had already tried to work in 1462 and 1463, but had then abandoned, convinced that no work of art could be made from a block of this size and shape.

Recently the subject of an act of vandalism, the *David* is now protected by barriers but these do not prevent us appreciating the full beauty of the piece.

Michelangelo, the 'Slave', Atlantis.

We now come to the first of the three *Florentine Rooms*, with many panel paintings from the early Florentine Renaissance. First is an extremely elegant cassone panel by a 15th-century Florentine artist, known as the master of the *Adimari Cassone*, today recognized to be Giovanni di ser Giovanni, also called Lo Scheggia (1406-1486), Massaccio's half-brother.

In 15th-century Florence these long chests replaced cupboards and clothes and household linen were kept in them.

They were therefore a traditional gift for newly-weds. The scene represents a wedding, which was erroneously believed to be that of Boccaccio Adimari and Lisa Ricasoli, and provides a rich source of information about contemporary costume and urban architecture. It is an image of Florentine life which documents the clothes and hairstyles fashionable in the 15th century.

Also in this room are paintings by Mariotto di Cristofano (1393-1457), Domenico di Michelino (1417-1491) and Andrea del Giusto (1424-1450). These artists absorbed the new style of art developed by Masaccio and Fra Angelico, though they lack the compositional expertise. Another artist of considerable ability was Cosimo Rossetti (1439-1507), whose workshop in Florence was renowned at the end of the 15th century. The *Annunciation* is from Lippi's workshop and its formal and figurative style reveal the presence of at least two different artists.

The room also houses other important paintings and it would be impossible to mention them all. They provide however, an unparalleled panorama of Florentine art and culture in this period.

The next two rooms are dedicated to late 15th-century Florentine painting. The period was much influenced by Botticelli, represented here by a panel with the *Virgin and Child*, *Pietà and Two angels*

Michelangelo, St. Matthew.

Lorenzo Monaco, Annunciation.

Micelangelo, the Palestrina Pietà.

Giovanni da Milano, Pietà.

(1475) from the hospital of Santa Maria Nuova in Florence.

There is also an elegant little *Visitation* next to the window which has been attributed to both Ghirlandaio and Perugino, though the latter artist now seems more likely.

The large painting on the end wall by Alessio Baldinovetti (1425-1499), the *Holy Trinity with Sts. Benedict and Giovanni Gualberto* (1471) has, however, lost much of its original colour.

To the right is a small painting of *Thebaid* in which fantastic and rational elements are so well balanced within an artificial perspective, that one inevitably thinks of the works of Paolo Uccello, who probably is the author of the work.

Michelangelo, David.

On the far wall of the third room is a *Resurrection* (c.1505) by a pupil of Filippino Lippi, Raffaellino del Garbo (1466-1524).

The dynamic use of colour and composition draws us into the scene which is set in highly contrasting, naturalistic surroundings.

To the right of the Tribune are the *Stories of the Martyr Saints* by Francesco Granacci (1469/70-1543); some clear, bright paintings by Ridolfo del Ghirlandaio, the beauty of which has been much improved by recent cleaning, and paintings by the Mannerists Alessandro Allori, Pontormo and Agnolo Bronzino demonstrating their wonderful compositional style.

The *Deposition* was commissioned from Bronzino by Grand Duke Cosimo. Painted between 1564 and 1565, according to the principles dictated by the artistic counter-reformation, the appalled and resigned expressions barely visible in the faces and gestures of the figures display an underlying emotive element, intended to move the observer. This eloquent work is, unfortunately, in poor condition. Finally, on the wall to the right of the David is a painting of *Venus* by the Florentine Mannerist painter, Pontormo.

The preparatory drawing was provided in 1533 by Michelangelo, an indication of the immense respect there was between the two artists. This is a scholarly painting, containing a wealth of cultural, iconographic references to matters of interest to learned Florentine circles at the time. On the left side of the left wing of the Tribune we enter the three *Sale Bizantine*, where various paintings, some from the second half of the 13th century, are housed.

In the first room on the right, on the right-hand wall, is the famous *Mary Magdalen* with scenes of her life (1280).

This is the work of a late 13th-century artist, master of a very active workshop, known as the Maestro della Maddalena, after this important work. Next is a *Madonna and Child with Saints*, by the Maestro di San Gaggio, dated the last decade of the 13th century. A certain animation in the figure, no longer so static and solemn, is already perceptible here, approaching the style of Giotto.

Looking again at the *Magdalen*, we see her facing front covered entirely with the long hair she grew while in the desert. In her hand she holds a scroll, with the writing "Sinners do not lose hope, follow my example and be reconciled with God".

Opposite the *Magdalen* is one of the most interesting works in the gallery: the *Tree of Life* (1310), by the Florentine painter Pacino di Bonaguida (active between 1303 and 1320).

This is an example of art in the form of the Poor Man's Bible, the illustrative representation of a written text. The work is based on an iconographic representation of Christ crucified on a tree with twelve branches, codified in the "Lignum Vitae" by the Franciscan monk Saint Bonaventure.

The painting develops in a way which is fascinating both for its inventiveness and its grace, revealing the artist's training as a miniaturist.

The second room, on the left, contains mid-13th century works

including those by the three Orcagna brothers, Andrea di Cione, *Michelangelo, David (detail).*
the oldest, Nardo and Jacopo.

Their workshop was one of the most famous in Florence from the
middle to the end of the 14th century. Andrea di Cione is the author
of the small and highly expressive polyptych portraying the Virgin
with *Sts. Andrew, Nicholas, John the Baptist and James* in the
centre, taken from Santissima Annunziata and dated mid-14th
century.

The artist has eliminated the divisions between the various parts
and, placing the figures lightly and delicately, he anticipates
developments in Florentine art during the 15th century.

The polyptych immediately beside, representing the *Holy Trinity*
(1365) between Saints Romuald and John the Evangelist, is by
Nardo, while the *Coronation of the Virgin*, (1379) immediately to
the right of the entrance, is by Jacopo.

Made for the Florentine mint, to which the gold background and
the rich decoration are an allusion, this is one of the most important
14th-century works for a public commission. The Renaissance
artist has here applied contemporary techniques to a medieval
interpretation of the subject, using, for example, the rules of
perspective on a gold ground.

The third room is to the right of the first and displayed here on the

Maestro del Cassone Adimari, the Adimari Cassone.

Andrea Rico da Candia, Virgin and Child.

far wall is a large polychrome *Cross* from the workshop of Bernardo Daddi. On the right is a fragment of the decoration on the *Armadio delle Reliquie*, once in the sacristy of Santa Croce, painted by Bernardo Daddi (c.1290-1348) who was a pupil of Giotto and one of the greatest artists of the century.

Lastly, to the left on the same wall, is a pointed panel painting of the *Pietà* (1365), a masterpiece by Giovanni da Milano. The elegant linear style belies the northern origins of the artist and he manages to interpret the scene by merely hinting at, rather than describing, the drama, leaving us quite enchanted.

The left wing of the Tribune houses distinguished works of the late-Mannerist and Baroque periods, by artists such as Alessandro Allori (1535-1607), Cosimo Gamberucci (c.1560-1621) and Poppi (1544-1597). From here we come to the *Salone delle Toscane*, originally the women's ward of the San Matteo hospital which, when the gallery was founded in 1784, was dedicated to 14th-century Tuscan painting. Today it houses 19th-century items and works related to the Accademia delle Belle Arti, including the collection of original models and plaster-casts made by Lorenzo Bertolini and Luigi Pampaloni. There are also paintings by Silvestro Lega, Ulisse Campi and Francesco Sabatelli. Many of these works are not only of high artistic quality, but are also important for their historical signifcance, such as the memorials to Machiavelli and Leon Battista Alberti, the portraits of Byron, Listz and Madame de Staël, and the sepulchral monument to Prince Anatolio Demidoff.

Returning along the corridor of the *Prisoners*, we come to the entrance.

From the stairs on the right we reach the first floor rooms, opened to the public in 1985. Between the two doors on the right is a *Tryptych* (1393-1404) by Mariotto di Nardo (active 1393-1424), a stylish Florentine painter of the early 15th century. Although he owed his considerable artistic ability to Andrea Orcagna, his style is still reminiscent of Giotto. There are also two polychrome *Crosses* of the same period by Lorenzo Monaco, the most important artist working in Florence between the Gothic and Renaissance periods.

The next large room houses various works by artists of the 14th and early 15th centuries: Lorenzo Monaco; Giovanni del Biondo (active from 1356 to 1392); Bicci di Lorenzo (1373-1452); Niccolò di Pietro Gerini (active 1399-1427); Spinello Aretino (c.1346-1410) and

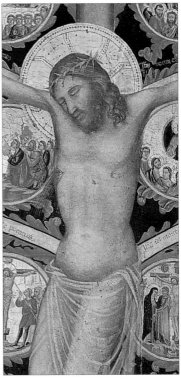

Pacino di Bonaguida,
Tree of Life and detail.

Andrea Orcagna. Some of these panels and triptychs have been integrated with later works. This room houses the greatest quantity of large polyptychs in a single location, in the world. On the wall on the right is the *Presentation at the Temple* (1363) by Giovanni del Biondo, taken from the convent of Santa Maria degli Angeli. This reveals the painter's narrative style, intended to render the religious theme more comprehensible.

Next is *Pentecost* (c.1470), accredited to Spinello Aretino by Vasari, though more probably painted in the workshop of Andrea Orcagna. The twelve disciples and the Virgin are cleverly arranged to fit them all into a limited space. Further ahead is a large polyptych of the *Coronation of the Virgin*, originally on the main altar of the Santa Felicità church in Florence. A record of 1399 attributes it to three artists, Spinello Aretino, Niccolò di Pietro Gerini and his son, Lorenzo di Niccolò.

On the wall at the far end of the room is one of the largest

Pontormo, Venus and Cupid.

polyptychs in existence: the *Annunciation* (1380-85) was made by Giovanni del Biondo for the Cavalcanti Altar in the sacristy of Santa Maria Novella. The wealth of detail in this work is impressive.

Also of note is the delicate painting, usually given the title of the *Annunciation* (1390-95), by the Maestro della Madonna Straus, whose soft, gentle tones are reminiscent of the works of Giovanni da Milano.

Up a few steps to the right is a series of paintings by Neri di Bicci, son of Bicci di Lorenzo, whose workshop was active in Florence towards the end of the 15th century. Displayed below these is the important collection of Russian icons, brought to Florence by the Lorraine, a present, perhaps, from Catherine of Russia to her godson, Pietro Leopoldo.

Particularly interesting is the late 16th-century *Menologio* in two parts, from Moscow. In this, the lives of the saints are arranged according to the Byzantine calendar (the first day of the year falls on the 1st of September) so that they can be read on the eve of their feast day. The two pieces show the saints from September to February and from March to August.

The last room in the Gallery is dedicated to Florentine late Gothic, the final examples of this style of art as the Renaissance period begins. The two great protagonists here are Lorenzo Monaco and Gherardo Starnina.

Monaco's famous *Annunciation* came from the Badia Fiorentina, while the small, pointed panel of the *Virgin and Child with Sts. John the Baptist and Nicola da Bari* is by Starnina.

Previous page: Orator.

François Vase (detail).

The museum is located in the Palazzo della Crocetta, built by Giulio Parigi in 1619-20, who enlarged an earlier lodge made for Lorenzo the Magnificent on land which he had bought here. In 1491 in fact, Giuliano da Sangallo (c.1444-1516) had already made plans for an enormous dynastic palace, between Via Capponi and Borgo Pinti, the main body of which would have been between Via Giusti and Viale Matteotti.

So enormous would this have been that the area now covered by the present Palazzo della Crocetta, would have been merely a garden terrace.

The plan was never carried out however, and more than a century later the Grand Duchess Maria Maddalena, sister of Cosimo II, took up residence in the family lodge. The Grand Duke ordered this building to be made for her and Parigi linked it by a passage to Santissima Annunziata and to the nearby Crocetta monastery in Via Laura. In 1621 the cloisters were extended right up to the palace, but on the death of the Grand Duchess in 1633, this became once more part of the private Medici residence. Various female members of the family lived here and it was also used as a guest house.

During the first decades of the rule of the Lorraine family, it became, on several occasions, the residence of the Regency. Further building and alterations were carried out in 1743, 1759-68, and in 1788, by Pietro Leopoldo who lived there for several months every year, and who finally took up residence in 1791 as Duke Leopoldo II.

In 1860 it was decided to house the Gallery of Modern Art here, but instead, during the period when Florence was capital of Italy, it became the seat of the *Corte dei Conti*. Further alterations therefore took place then, and yet again in 1879 when it was decided to house the Archeological Museum here.

In 1884 a collection of tapestries was hung on the second floor, but they were removed in 1925. The buildings around the garden were altered and extended in 1908 and again in 1929-40. In 1942 the ex-Innocenti Palazzo on Piazza Santissima Annunziata was acquired and a new entrance was made here, but abandoned after the flood of November 4th, 1966.

The oldest collecton in the museum is that begun by the Medici, who were interested in antiquities of all kinds. In the 18th century the Grand Dukes of Lorraine continued to protect this branch of archeology with specific laws.

The museum really flourished, however, in the 19th century when Leopoldo II created a completely new Egyptian Museum to house the wealth of artefacts brought back from Egypt by the Tuscan expedition of Ippolito Rossellini.

This was first housed in Via Santa Caterina (1832) and then in the Cenacolo di Fuligno (1851) where, in 1871, the Etruscan collection was also located. Finally in 1879 it was decided to provide all these collections with more suitable accommodation in the Palazzo della Crocetta. This transfer was organized by the palaeographer, Luigi Pigorini who also re-arranged the collections which had grown considerably in the meantime.

In 1897 the Topographical Museum was opened and for this Adriano Milani, the director of the Egyptian Museum, decided to create a new system of classification, bringing all the items together in one chronological and geographical sequence.

In 1903 a new architectural section was created consisting of the reconstructed Etruscan tombs in the garden of the building.

The repair and restoration of the museum still continues today, and is carried out according to the latest techniques. This can be seen from the delicate Neo-classical decoration, dating from the time of the Lorraine, discovered during the strengthening of the walls and ceilings on the second floor.

The decorations are almost all geometric except for one completely restored ceiling with a floral design. The pastel shades range from pink to green and the palest yellow and a correct colour contrast has been left between the original parts and those which have been restored.

The present arrangement is still experimental. The museum's vast wealth of possessions can usually only be visited with a guide, and the itinerary is constantly changed.

Room I is immediately after the ticket office: in the centre of the room is the famous *François Vase*, a volute krater, made in Athens and dated 575 B.C. The decorative friezes in the central part of the vase illustrate the marriage of the parents of Achilles, Thetis and Peleus, attended by the Greek gods of Olympus.

There are six other decorative horizontal bands, with antique mythological scenes. Each character is easily identified by the inscription beside them. The decoration is of black figures, using a graffito technique with overpainting, some of which has disappeared. The François Vase is named after the archeologist who discovered it in pieces in an Etruscan tomb near Chiusi (Siena) in 1845. In 1973 it underwent a lengthy and difficult process of restoration in order to eliminate the many pieces which had been integrated into it by 19th-century restorers.

The stages in this restoration and re-assemblage are well documented in the illustrated panels around the walls.

The Idolino bronze statue.

Hydra with Aphrodite and Phaon.

Relief of the goddess Maat.

In Room II are beautiful examples of cinerary statues from Chiusi in tufaceous stone.

The ashes or possessions of the dead were stored inside the statues, which are in the form of male and female figures with removeable heads.

On the right is the *Mater Matuta*, so called because it was believed to represent a goddess of fertility or maternity, though today it is thought to be simply a female figure holding a child.

Discovered at Chianciano during the last century, the statue is in tufaceous stone and may be dated to the middle of the 5th century B.C. Beside the Mater Matuta is an alabaster sarcophagus with the deceased and his wife portrayed in a banqueting scene according to typical Etruscan iconography of the 5th century B.C.

The husband holds a patera or chalice of coloured alabaster in his hand. On the left is a sarcophagus of painted terracotta from Chiusi. This is named after the deceased woman, *Larthia Seianti*, who is portrayed drawing back a veil from her face in order to see herself better in the mirror she holds in her left hand. This beautiful piece is dated between 175 and 150 B.C. and is comparable to many of the pieces conserved in the British Museum in London.

Continuing, we reach Room III, or the *Milani Room*, named after the doner of the two antique *Kouroi* displayed here, the *Apollo* and the *Milani Young Apollo*, two nude figures of young men, standing.

The first is in marble and the legs beneath the knees are damaged. It may be dated around 530 B.C. due to the smile, a means of lending expression to the face which was not used in the later, more severe period.

To the left of the entrance is a neo-Attic relief of the 2nd-1st century B.C., a copy of a Phidian frieze found on the throne of the statue of Zeus in Olympia. It illustrates the *Murder of the Children of Niobe* by *Apollo and Artemis*.

Returning to the museum entrance, the stairs lead to the upper floors. On the first floor, to the right, is the Etruscan, Greek and Roman Collection (Rooms IX and X, XII-XV). On the left is the Egyptian Collection, donated to the museum by Ippolito Rossellini, who went on the Franco-Tuscan expedition to Egypt with Jean-François Champillon, famous for having deciphered hieroglyphics.

In rooms IX and X are many examples of Etruscan tomb sculptures, mainly discovered in Chuisi, Volterra and Perugia, the most important centres of production of funerary urns and sarcophagi.

The materials used were alabaster, tufa or travertine, and terracotta, with bas-relief decorations once painted with bright colours, now unfortunately lost. The covers of almost all the urns represent the deceased and his wife half-lying and usually in a banqueting pose. The faces are not actual portraits although they all appear to be different. The most famous and exemplary of all the urns in these two rooms is the *Amazon Sarcophagus*, in Asian marble, from Tarquinia. The two long sides are painted in tempera with scenes of the *Battle of Amazonia*, relating various stories.

The front panels of the cover are decorated in bas-relief, while engraved on the sloping sides of the sarcophagus are the names of the deceased woman (Ramtha Huzcnai) and her son (Larth Apaiatru). It is dated about 350 B.C., a period of considerable Greek and Italic influence on Etruscan art.

Many small mirrors and items of Etruscan toilette are displayed in the cases in Room XIII. The backs of these are decorated with Greek mythical scenes, engraved with the names of the characters.

The most famous of these is, without doubt, the mirror representing *Hercules being Suckled by Juno* (3rd century B.C.), discovered at Volterra and indicated by the inventory number 72740. At the bottom is the figure of a kneeling sprite who seems to support the scene; in the central part is the scene of Hercules and Juno seated enthroned, while Jupiter (holding a sceptre), Apollo (holding a laurel branch), Venus and Minerva observe the scene. An upper band with the half-lying figure of a satyr completes the decoration.

The writing on a small scroll, held by Jupiter, has been thus interpreted: "this shows Hercules as the son of Juno". Though the figures still seem to have Greek characteristics, the details of hair style and jewels in the female characters are clearly Etruscan.

Mater Matuta.

Portrait of a Young Woman.

This room also houses the *Bronzo d'Idolino*, the name generally given to the famous statue of a young boy, once used as a lamp-stand for illuminating banquets. When it was discovered, the vines which he holds in the left hand lead to the belief that it represented Dionysus.

For this reason the 16th-century pedestal, attributed to Girolamo Lombardo, a sculptor from Ferrara, is decorated with motifs related to the cult of the god Dionysus. The vines held by the figure were detached in 1768, and it was the German archeologist, Rumpf, who interpreted the subject correctly, identifying it as being a Roman copy of Greek statues from the Polycletian period and dating it between the 1st century B.C. and the 1st century A.D.

Returning to Room XI, we find a long corridor on the left, Room XIV. The cases contain devotional bronzes, votive figures of animals, or of Greek, Roman and Etruscan religious figures from the antique, classical and Hellenistic periods.

These were mainly found in the graves of sacrifices made to the cults of various pagan gods. Between the first two cases, is the statue of the *Arezzo Minerva*, named after the town where it was found by chance in 1541. The right arm is the result of a repair carried out in 1785, which slightly altered the composition.

The statue is, in fact, probably a copy of an original by Praxiteles, which had the right hand close to the body, holding a lance.

Continuing, we come to another important Etruscan bronze, also from Arezzo, and one of the most important and famous pieces in the entire collection, the *Chimera*. Dated between the middle of the 5th century B.C. and the middle of the 4th century B.C., it was found just outside one of the city gates of Arezzo and was immediately added to Cosimo I's prestigious collection. An inscription on the front right paw indicates its votive function, though it tells us nothing about the

The Arezzo Chimera.

supplicant.

The Chimera probably represents the mythical beast with three heads (lion, snake and goat) with a lion's body. As legend relates, the animal was wounded several times by the spear of the hero Bellerophon, and the artist has succeeded in communicating the tension and power of the monsterous animal in extremis.

For a period of several centuries, many important workshops were active in the area around Arezzo and it was here that the famous statue of the *Orator* was produced. This Etruscan piece from the 1st century B.C. was found in the south of Tuscany, near to Lake Trasimeno. The statue, much influenced by Roman art, portrays the Orator Aule Metelli in Roman clothes.

At the back, on the hem of his toga is an Etruscan inscription dedicated to the "father god", much venerated in the area where it was found.

In Room XV are items from the grand-ducal collection, and some later aquisitions, dating from the late bronze age (10th century B.C.) to the late Middle Ages (7th century A.D.). As well as firearms and weapons there are scientific instruments and boxes for cosmetic items.

Room I begins the collection of artefacts in the Egyptian Museum. The arrangement is presently being reorganized. The collection consists of Egyptian items of various origin, covering a period of time from pre-historic to approximately 1700 B.C.

The items range from the most basic to the most elaborate, such as the vases dating from 5,000 to 3,000 B.C., decorated with geometric and natural motifs. In case number 11, are two little figures of servants carved in limestone, with well-preserved painted decorations: in one a woman is wringing out loaves of barley bread, fermented in a date liqueur, to make a kind of beer, while another is occupied in making bread: both items were believed to be vital food for the deceased in the other world.

In case number 12 is a *funerary stele* in the shape of a door, with an image of the deceased in the centre; it is of particular interest for the hieroglyphic writing.

Room II contains important examples of Egyptian stele of various origin, dated between 2040 and 1700 B.C. Somewhat unusual for the greater attention to natural detail are those of the XII dynasty (c.1840-1650 B.C.).

An example of this is the *commemorative stele* (inventory number 2540) on the far wall, to the left, portraying the Emporer Sesastris I celebrating his victories. Case number 6 contains a series of wooden statues of women, which are thought to represent the "concubines of the dead", which, like the models of boats and servants, were part of the tomb furnishings.

On the shelf below are *boomerangs* in bone and ivory, decorated with real and imaginary animals, dated 2160-1785 B.C. These were not only burial items, but were also used in hunting and in some specific religious ceremonies, to drive away evil spirits.

Room III houses objects datable to the period 1552 to 1186 B.C. On the

left is a statue in grey granite of the *Priest Ptahmose*, represented in   *Sarcophagus of Larthia Seanti.*
a pose which was characteristic during the XVIII dynasty (1400 B.C.).
Inside a case on the wall is a portrait of a young woman.

Such portraits were used by the Egyptians to cover the head of the
mummy, instead of the funeral mask, in Roman times. It is therefore a
life-like portrait of a later period, dated between the 1st and 2nd
centuries A.D., found in the necropolis at Fayum, near Cairo. Here the
dry atmosphere helped to preserve the paint and wood perfectly.

In cases 2 and 3 are other examples of painting. These contain
fragments of wall painting, taken from tombs of the XVIII Theban
dynasty, found in the Valley of the Kings.

The pieces are of a rare beauty and are perfectly preserved. The
wooden *War Chariot* on the right side of the room was found in a
Theban tomb of the XVIII dynasty (1552.1306 B.C.). It is unique in the
world and is the pride of the collection.

Until recently it was believed to be a model, with a purely funereal
function, but recent research has revealed signs of use on the rings for
the horses reins, thus showing that the occupant of the tomb used it
while still alive and it only later accompanied him to his grave.

Displayed in a series of cases to the right in Room IIb, are amulets
dating from 1070-333 B.C.

Made in various shapes and materials, these were worn round the
neck and were believed to bring good luck to both the living and the
dead.

Further ahead is some jewellery with gold pendants. Some of these,
set with ancient Egyptian stones, are 19th-century re-creations. In
Rooms IV and V are items of various origin from the New Kingdom.
Room VI houses items mainly from Thebes, such as the two large
mummy-shaped sarcophagi with idealized portrait masks.

From a different location are the papyri in panels ABC on the wall,

Orator.

Handle on the lid of an urn.

belonging to the *Book of the Dead*, which, if observed by the dead would, it was believed, ensure them of an afterlife. They are beautifully decorated in gold.

These cases also contain papyri over 4,000 years old. In cases 17 and 18 in Room VII are some small wooden statues.

These are usually referred to as 'ushabti', from the Egyptian word 'usceb' which means 'to reply'. Each tomb contained 365, one for every day of the year, and their function was to help their master by fulfilling his requests each day.

Room VIII contains various examples of mummies, some still with their bindings, inside their sarcophagus, though others are unwrapped. The most interesting is that of the young girl Takerheb, dating from the time of Ptolemy (332-30 B.C.). The process used to achieve the perfect mummification of a body was quite complex. Firstly the internal organs were removed, the body was de-hydrated with carbonate and sodium bi-carbonate and was then left in the sun for a considerable length of time. The inside was then filled with bandages, precious oils were sprinkled over the entire body and finally it was wrapped in linen bindings.

The two central cases in room XI contain bronzes and Greek terracotta figures (c.300 B.C.) representing people of all kinds, including those who were never portrayed during the classical period: old people, dwarves, hunch-backs, the deformed and the grotesque.

Lastly we come to the large room overlooking Piazza Santissima Annunziata.

This room previously housed the Topographical Museum which is to be totally reorganized. In the meantime it is used for frequent exhibitions. Before leaving, it is worth taking a look at the archeological garden, with steles, ancient boundary stones, statues and complete tomb chambers.

QVAB CONSVMATI SVNT DIES OCTO VT CIRCVCIDERET P̄   II.C.

NGAVI FVGIENS 7 MANSI INSOLITVDINE

GE ACCIPE PVERVM 7 MATREM EIᵽ 7 FVGE INEGIPTVM .MACEI.II.C.

The Museum of San Marco houses one of the most exceptional art collections in the city. Located in the delightful setting of this Dominican monastery is an important collection of art and sculpture, the greatest works being the paintings and frescoes of Fra Angelico.

Initially, the church and monastery of San Marco belonged to the order of the Silvestrines but in 1434 Pope Eugene IV entrusted it to the Dominicans. The entire complex was, however, in extremely poor condition and Cosimo Il Vecchio ordered that it should be restored and enlarged. This work was carried out between 1437 and 1452 by Michelozzo who designed a simple and harmonious building according to Renaissance principles.

Work was started first on the cells, and then on the cloisters of San Antonino, the Chapter House, and the Library. In the meantime the church was finished and consecrated, and then finally the cloister of San Domenico was completed. During this renovation Brother Giovanni from Fiesole, otherwise known as Fra Angelico, frescoed the monks' cells, the Chapter House, the lunettes in the cloisters and the refectory. Unfortunately the refectory was destroyed in 1554.

The monastery was suppressed in 1866, and in 1870 the building

Previous page: Fra Angelico, the Flight into Egypt.

Fra Angelico, Tabernacolo dei Linaioli.

Fra Angelico, Crucifixion with Saints.

became a museum housing almost all the works of Fra Angelico remaining in Florence, altogether about one hundred panels and frescoes. The museum was further extended in 1983 when a room was dedicated to Fra Bartolomeo and another to Baldovinetti.

Fra Angelico, San Marco Altarpiece.

Fra Angelico, Annalena Altarpiece.

The entrance is to the right of the church and the hall brings us into the main cloister. This is called after San Antonino, a Dominican monk of this monastery, who in 1466 became the best-loved and respected Bishop in the history of Florence. The cloister, designed by Michelozzo, is a quadrangle with a portico of low arches supported by Ionic columns on plinths. The internal lunettes were frescoed in the period from 1602 to the end of that century with scenes from the life of San Antonino by various artists. It thus constitutes an exceptional gallery of Baroque Florentine painting. From here one can also see the *Piagnona*, the bell tower of the monastery which rang calling in vain the citizens of Florence to the defence of Girolamo Savonarola when he was condemned to be burnt at the stake. It was thus nicknamed the 'piagnone' (the moaner) after the followers of Savonarola who denounced the sin of luxury and even enjoyment.

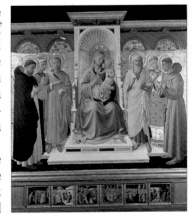

In the large room on the ground floor, the *Ospizio dei Pellegrini*, the works of Fra Angelico which were taken from various Florentine churches are exhibited. Fra Angelico was one of the most important Renaissance artists, able to understand Masaccio's innovations and interpret them in his own characteristic style while also applying the rules of perspective. He devoted his exceptional compositional and

Fra Angelico, Deposition.

Fra Angelico, Lamentation.

representational ability entirely to the service of the church. Immediately on the left is the *Tabernacolo dei Linaioli* (1433), made for the Linen Drapers Guild. Inside an elaborate marble frame, designed by Ghiberti, is the earliest attributed work by Angelico. On the outer side of the doors are *St. Mark* on the left, and *St. Peter*, while on the predella beneath are *St. Peter Preaching*, the *Adoration of the Magi* and the *Martyrdom of St. Mark*. In the centre is the *Madonna and Child* and on the inside of the doors are *St. John the Baptist* on the left and *St. John the Evangelist*. In this work we can see that the artist is moving towards stylstic maturity.

Continuing along the wall of the entrance is the famous *San Marco Altarpiece* dated 1438-40. This was commissioned from Fra Angelico for the main altar in the church of San Marco by Cosimo de' Medici whose portrait can be seen in the figure of St. Cosmas. Looking at it more closely we can see that the paintwork is much deteriorated. Serious damage was caused in the past by cleaning with sodium carbonate which irrevocably damaged the original pigment of the paint and even the work of restoration carried out in 1955 was unable to save or improve the quality. Despite its faded nature, the work is still one of the most impressive and magnificent altarpieces of the 15th century. The flourishing landscape seen beyond the wood, between the trunks of the cedar and cypress trees is still extremely beautiful and was probably influenced by the innovations seen in contemporary Flemish art. Displayed opposite this are the three *Scenes from the Life of Christ*, by Alessio Baldovinetti.

On the same wall is the lovely *Annalena Altarpiece*, called after the monastery for which it was painted, San Vincenzo di Annalena, in Florence. This is the oldest known Renaissance altarpiece. No longer divided into a triptych, the scene is painted as a single piece against a

clearly Renaissance architectural background, using clear and bright colours. The way in which the saints are arranged is quite innovative, placed around the Madonna in a semi-circle in relaxed and conversational poses, causing the work to be described as one of the first Renaissance 'Sacre conversazioni'.

On the far wall is the *Deposition* (1435-40), painted for the Strozzi Chapel in the Santa Trinità church in Florence. The central part shows the body of Christ deposed and at his feet a kneeling believer, possibly Alessio degli Strozzi. On the left we see the pious women with the Virgin and on the right are some male figures. The landscapes in the background are so entirely realistic that they are surprizing in the work of an artist whose main motivation was religious. There are many other paintings in this room and some of the smaller ones, executed with an almost miniaturist technique, may be dated 1433-35. On the wall opposite the second door is, firstly, a beautiful *Deposition* (1436), painted for the Florentine Confraternity of Santa Maria della Croce al Tempio, then a small panel of the *Naming of John the Baptist*. Finally is one of Fra Angelico's masterpieces, the *Universal Judgement* (1431-35), painted on the back of a lectern used for religious ceremonies which accounts for its unusual shape. Commissioned in 1431 for the Florentine monastery of Santa Maria degli Angeli, the work was conceived in a most original manner, depite its medieval theme. The artist has used 14th-century symbolism, reinterpreting it however, according to Renaissance principles. This can be seen, for example, in the perspective of the open tomb in the hemicycle of saints at the top, around Christ in judgement. The whole scene is somewhere between an enlarged miniature and a small fresco and has been painted with great care and attention to detail. This can be seen in the host of the chosen, who are turning towards Christ, or are in a ring with angels in the flower garden in front of the gates of Paradise, bathed in the light of grace.

Lastly, on leaving the room, are panels from the *Armadio degli Argenti* from Santissima Annunziata, containing some lively *Scenes from the Life of Christ*, painted about 1450. Some of the most famous scenes in the series are the *Annunciation, the Nativity, the Flight into*

Egypt, and the *Slaughter of the Innocents*. Displayed in a case is an illuminated manuscript and alongside are some examples of script and decorated initials.

Before proceeding to the first floor, we pass through the *Sala del Lavabo* where the monks sprinkled themselves with holy water before entering the refectory. Various works are displayed here and one should note the *Tabernacle* by the school of Della Robbia and the *Predella* believed to be an early work by Paolo Uccello.

In the next room, known as the *Fra Bartolomeo Room* is the large altarpiece of the *Madonna and St. Anne* also known as the *Signoria Altarpiece* (c.1512). This excellent monochrome was painted for the church of San Lorenzo by Baccio della Porta, and provides an important insight into the techniques and preparatory methods used in 16th-century painting.

Above the door is the *Final Judgement* (1499-1501) by Fra Bartolomeo, finished however, by Mariotto Albertinelli and brought here from Santa Maria Nuova. The composition of the upper part of this large fresco gave Raphael the idea for his *Disputa*.

The room on the right is the *Refectory*. This large room was part of the original late 14th-century structure of the Silvestrine monastery and it now houses works of the 16th, 17th and 18th centuries, such as the *Crucifixion with Mourners and Mary Magdalen* by Lorenzo Lippi (1606-1655) and panel paintings by Giovanni Antonio Sogliani (1492-1544). On the far wall is a large fresco by Sogliani showing the Dominican monks at table, watched over by the large *Crucifixion* in the background.

Next is the *Saletta del Baldovinetti* with works by Benozzo Gozzoli, Cosimo Rosselli (1439-1507) and Antoniazzo Romano (1461-1508). Also

Fra Angelico, *Transfiguration of Christ*.

Fra Angelico, *Annunciation (in corridor)*.

Fra Angelico, *Annunciation*.

View of the Campanile.

here is a painting of *St. Antonino at the Foot of the Cross*, in a magnificent frame with fruits and garlands, previously in the church of San Marco.

In the middle of the northern side of the cloisters is the *Chapter House*, where the monks met on important ceremonial days and for theological and doctrinal discussions. The wall opposite the door is completely frescoed with the *Crucifixion and Saints* by Fra Angelico (1442-43). The subject is treated in an original manner, almost like a mystical vision: as well as those characters present at the scene according to the gospels, there are also numerous other saints, including the Fathers of the Church, renowned Dominicans and founders of famous orders. The work is quite majestic: the figures are placed in front of an empty space, lending them greater compositonal solidity and force, heightened by the fact that the cycle has become reddish in colour, due to the loss of the lapis-lazuli blue.

We now reach the first floor: immediately at the top of the stairs is one of Fra Angelico's best known paintings, the *Annunication* (1437). The scene is bathed in a marvellous light and takes place under a loggia opening out onto a field covered with flowers and separated by a fence from a garden full of luxuriant, leafy trees.

Compared to the other frescoes in the cells, this is more decorative in style, probably to emphasize its more formal role, while the others, given their more private function, are slightly humbler. Almost opposite the *Annunciation* at the other end of the corridor, is a fresco of *San Domenico in Worship at the Cross*.

Starting with the first corridor on the left, each cell is decorated with a different fresco. There is no established order to them as the religious subjects illustrated are not chronological in order. Their intention was simply to encourage the monks in their contemplation and meditation. In each cell Fra Angelico represented the mysteries of Christianity whether joyful, glorious or sorrowful, as a continual reminder that man has a noble destiny.

In the first cell on the left, the wall opposite the door is frescoed with a *Noli Me Tangere*, with the risen Christ appearing to Mary Magdalen in a tranquil woodland scene. The second cell has a *Lamentation*, while the third is decorated with another masterpiece, an *Annunciation*. The simplicity of the scene, the elimination of any decorative element and the lack of symbolism combine to create a great spiritual and artistic work. Next, in the fourth cell, is a *Crucifixion*, a *Nativity* is in the fifth and a splendid *Transfiguation of Christ* in the sixth, half way along the corridor. This large fresco is particularly interesting: within a brilliant oval shape a solemn and sculptural figure of Christ is depicted in bright clothes. He looks sympathetically towards mankind, represented by the figures of three apostles who are perturbed by the sudden glare, but are anxious to reach the divine light.

The seventh cell portrays a symbolic *Crowning with Thorns*, while the next contains the *Two Marys and San Domenico at the Tomb*. In the ninth cell is the *Coronation of the Virgin*, a theme frequently painted by the artist but dealt with here in an original manner, representing

the scene within a circle of divine light. In the communicating tenth and eleventh cells are respectively, a *Presentation of Christ at the Temple* and a *Virgin Enthroned*. The former is the last fresco unanimously attributed to Fra Angelico. In fact the frescoes in the following cells do not seem to have been carried out directly by him. It is possible that he left the completion of the work to a series of assistants such as Zanobi Strozzi (1412-1471) and Benozzo Gozzoli (1420-1497), though the marvellous design and composition lead us to believe that he left a precise and detailed plan of the work, possibly even preparing the synopsis himself.

We see these cells returning down the corridor. The first is particularly interesting as, in addition to the fresco of the *Crucifixion with the Virgin*, we can also see, with the help of glass and mirrors, some medieval murals beneath the floor. The next rooms are frescoed with the following themes: the *Crucifixion of Christ with Angels*, the *Baptism of Christ*, the *Crucifixion with San Domenico*, the *Virgin Enthroned with Child* (this is on the outer wall, in the corridor), the *Resurrection with Symbols of the Passion*; the *Flagellation*, the *Road to Calvary*, and lastly, two *Crucifixions with the Madonna and San Domenico*.

We now come to the entrance corridor. Here we find the cell of Sant'Antonino with the *Descent of Christ into Limbo*, two double cells (the first with the *Sermon on the Mount* and the *Temptation*, the second traditionally thought to be Fra Angelico's with the *Entry to Jerusalem*), the *Sermon in the Garden*, a *Madonna*, and a *Santa Marta*, the *Communion of the Disciples* and a *Crucifixion*. Next is a small cell with an entrance chamber frescoed with *Christ Crucified between the Thieves*. Opposite are the two cells reserved for Cosimo Il Vecchio's retreats, and where Pope Eugene IV also stayed when the church of San Marco was consecrated in 1443. In the entrance is a *Crucifixion*, a *Madonna*, a St. *Peter Martyr*, *St. John* and *St. Cosma*. Up a few steps inside the cell with a skylight, is an *Epiphany*. There are 43 cells altogether and the last three contain *Longino and the*

Domenico Ghirlandaio, Last Supper.

*Domenico Ghirlandaio,
Last Supper (detail).*

Lance and *Sts. Paolo, Domenico, Maria and Marta*, in the first, a *Crucifixion* in the second and some small paintings of *St. Domenico* in the third.

Between the last two cells is an entrance to the Library, a beautiful room designed by Michelozzo in 1448. This long hall is divided into three aisles with arches on columns with Ionic capitals, a barrel vault ceiling in the middle and cross vault ceilings to the sides. The cases display rare Antiphonals and Psalm Books, decorated with excellent miniatures.

From the corridor we return to the ground floor. To the right, at the bottom of the stairs is the small Refectory, with some Della Robbia terracottas and a recently restored *Last Supper* (1480) by Domenico Ghirlandaio. This is one of Ghirlandaio's most important works, portraying the scene in a narrative manner, free of anxiety or tragic emotion. He also makes excellent use of the architectural structure of the room with the real and his painted vaults fusing into one, using the same technique as that in the *Last Supper* of the Refectory in Ognissanti. The naturalistic and descriptive style, full of symbols and Christian iconography (birds, a peacock, a cat and vase of lilies), represent the influence of Flemish realism which had arrived in Florence with the *Portinari Tripytch* by Hugo Van der Goes.

Leaving this room we come to a corridor where some architectural stonework is displayed. The Guest House and lastly the adjacent small cloister of the Silvestrines, house a museum which is not very well-known, but is of especial interest for the city of Florence. The Museum of Old Florence was reorganized and arranged in 1990 and houses records and items relevant to the old city centre. Displayed here are artefacts saved during the work of demolition which took place between 1885-1890: architectural elements, family coats of arms, tabernacles, doorways and frescoes taken from private houses are displayed and accompanied by photographs and explanations. Some of the most interesting pieces are, for example, the early Christian sarcophagus, sculpted with episodes from the life of Jonah, re-used in the 14th century by the Teri family who had their own coat of arms engraved on it; the *tomb sculpture* of Bishop Vincenzo Trinci, with the deceased portrayed in a lying position, and a commemorative plaque with an inscription (1489-1491) by Guisto di Giovanni da Settignano and Clemente di Taddeo da Santa Maria a Pontanico.

Before leaving from the garden, we can see the rear view of the church of San Marco, framed by small arches, and Michelozzo's slender bell tower, with its elegant bell chamber and its pyramid-shaped pinnacle.

THE MEDICI
CHAPELS

Previous page: Michelangelo, Day.

Michelangelo, Madonna and Child.

The generic name of the Medici Chapels includes the Chapel of the Princes and the New Sacristy, which, together with the Laurentian Library, form the buildings of the church of San Lorenzo.

According to some, the Chapel of the Princes had already been planned by Cosimo I though it was commissioned and built by Ferdinando I who proclaimed a competition for it in 1602.

The ambitious project was carried out between 1605 and 1640 by the architect Matteo Nigetti (1560-1649), based on the plans, already partially altered by Buontalenti, of Don Giovanni de' Medici, illegitimate son of Cosimo and winner of the competition.

This lavish creation is one of the few examples of Florentine Baroque. It took more than three hundred years to complete the project which was undertaken by the Opificio delle Pietre Dure using precious and costly materials.

Most of the wall covering and decoration was completed during the 17th and 18th centuries, though the altar was completed, in the face of much criticism, in 1939.

The floor was only completed in 1962.

In 1913 a new independent entrance to these sumptuous, self-aggrandizing mausoleums was opened, thus avoiding the flux of the large number of visitors passing through the church.

The visit begins in the spacious and interesting *Crypt* (1508) designed by Buontalenti. Many members of the Medici and Lorraine families are buried here, and their tombstones can be seen in the floor.

The vaults are supported by low, sturdy columns and one can almost sense here the impending weight of the chapels above. Beneath the crypt, but not open to the public, is the basement designed by Brunelleschi with the tombs of Cosimo Il Vecchio and Donatello.

Stairs on the right lead to the *Chapel of the Princes*. The chamber is extremely large, fascinating yet overpowering. It is of octagonal design, with a domed ceiling, frescoed in 1828 by Pietro Benvenuti (1769-1844) with *Stories from the Old and New Testaments*, as well as *Prophets* and *Disciples*.

The walls and furnishings are entirely in dark shades of marble and semi-precious stone, reminiscent of the theme of death, albeit with the hope of after-life.

Around the bottom of the walls is a series of sixteen coats of arms belonging to the cities of the Grand Duchy of Tuscany.

These fine pieces of semi-precious stone inlay were made in the 17th century using lapis-lazuli, mother of pearl, and coral.

Around the walls are the six monumental sarcophagi of the Grand Dukes Ferdinando II, Cosimo II, Ferdinando I, Cosimo I, Francesco I and Cosimo III, surmounted by crowns on cushions and tabernacles with niches.

The second and third sarcophagi also have large gilded bronze statues of the relevant Grand Dukes, made by Pietro (1577-1640) and Ferdinando (1616/19-1686) Tacca.

Behind the altar in marble and pietradura are the two sacristies, the

Chapel of the Princes.

Chapels of the Relics and of the Treasury.
These house reliquaries of various periods (15th and 16th century) and items from the Treasury of San Lorenzo. Originally these were brought out to be venerated on certain religious festivals, and were kept in the tribune of the inner façade of the church itself, designed by Michelangelo. Note in particular, on the left of the altar the delicate *Pastoral* in gilded silver, a gift from Pope Leo X to the church in 1520. It is most finely made with a half figure of San Lorenzo inside the curl and heads of lions and Medici coats of arms in the 'knots'.
Also worthy of note are the 16th-century, Florentine *Reliquary-bust* of St. Anne in painted wood and the *Mitre*, decorated with pearls and jewels, displaying the Medici coat of arms, also a gift from Leo X, and

lastly the sumptuous 17th-century *Reliquary*, decorated with flowers and fronds, containing a bone of St. Casimir of Lithuania. In the cases are many Greek, Roman and medieval vases made of rock crystal, amethyst and jasper, containing relics.

These came from Lorenzo the Magnificent's collection and were donated to the church by his second son, Pope Leo X.

Returning to the Chapel of the Princes, we pass through the narrow corridor which houses two marble 'Trophies' of warriors arms, probably school of Michelangelo and displayed in the Uffizi until the 18th century.

According to one of Michelangelo's first plans, these would have been positioned above the tombs of the Dukes. The corridor brings us into

Octagonal cupola of the chapel.

Michelangelo, the tombs of Giuliano and Lorenzo, Duke of Urbino.

Michelangelo's first architectural work, the *New Sacristy*.

The name of the chapel distinguishes it from the *Old Sacristy* by Brunelleschi, of which it is a continuation and counterpart, being in a position symmetrical to it. Commissioned by cardinal Giulio de' Medici and Pope Leo X, Michelangelo worked on it from 1521 to 1534 with various interruptions. When, however, he left Florence forever, Cosimo I ordered it to be completed by Vasari and Ammannati and it was finished about 1555. The shape of the interior has an amazing impact. The plan is square with a domed ceiling.

The tricks of perspective, the glimpses of the lofty space above and the effect of the walls divided by double pilasters, providing the backdrop to the funereal monuments, all create a most unusual setting.

To the left, above the sarcophagus with *Dawn* (1524-27) and *Dusk* (1524-31) is a statue of *Lorenzo de' Medici* (1525), Duke of Urbino and grandson of Lorenzo the Magnificent.

Vasari endowed Lorenzo with the characteristic of Thoughtfulness, even if historically his image is identified as representing the contemplation of tryanny.

Coats of arms of the Medicean cities around the chapel walls.

The symbolic objects with which he is portrayed have also been interpreted in various ways: the helmet with the lion's head is seen as a symbol of strength, the casket of coins is seen either as a symbol of parsimony or as an image of death, and the item in his left hand is either a small purse or a handkerchief.

The statue of *Dawn* is on the right of the sarcophagus, paired with *Dusk* on the left. The former is portrayed as a young woman in the act of reluctantly awakening, while the latter is an older man who seems to accept rest with a hint of sadness.

Both were inspired by antiquity, in particular by personifications of river gods. They may be seen as symbolizing time or the humours of the spirit, indicating 'time which passes for all', the human drama of the rapid passage of time.

The tombs were recently cleaned and this has brought to light the way in which Michelangelo originally dealt with the marble surface, working it with gradine and chisel and polishing it according to the light and shade. The work which thus emerged is like a painted sculpture, similar and parallel to the sculptural paintings so typical of Michelangelo.

On the opposite wall is the sarcophgus with *Night* (1526-31) and *Day* (1526-31), above which is the sculpture of *Giuliano de' Medici* (1526-34), the Duke of Nemours, Lorenzo the Magnificent's third son.

Both this and the statue of Lorenzo were completed by Giovanni Montorsoli (c.1507-1536) who did not, however, alter the composition.

Giuliano is dressed in classical armour, ready for action and endowed with pride of spirit. In contrast to Lorenzo, he is seen as representing a life of action, a strong-willed and violent despot.

The symbols he holds have been interpreted differently too: the staff is symbolic of the church and the coins in his hand may be a sign of generosity.

The *figure of Night* on the left of the tomb was one of the first pieces

Michelangelo, Night.

to be started for the sacristy and one of the first to be completed. This female figure in anguished concentration is rich in allegorical symbolism such as the diadem, the owl, the poppy and the mask which may be interpreted as references to dreams, nightmares or sensuality, while its significance refers to the cosmic symbolism of the fertility of night. The tragic face of the statue of *Day* on the right is sculpted in Michelangelo's disturbing 'non-finito' style, relating it closely to the *Prisoners* and the *Prophets* in the Sistine Chapel.

The male figure is writhing in a movement almost of rebellion and *Day* is in fact interpreted as the personification of pain, freedom, anger, vendetta. In relation to the other statues of the sacristy it is symbolic of the element of fire.

Both these personifications represent the eternal problems created by thought and human action.

On the wall to the right of the door is the statue of the *Madonna and Child* (1521-34) with the statues of Sts. Cosmas and Damian above the simple casket-shaped sarcophagus. One of Michelangelo's master-pieces, the *Madonna and Child* is the fulcrum towards which the eyes and thoughts of the two princes, seated on their tombs, seem to turn and is thus the ideal point of convergence for the entire structure.

The hope of redemption and eternal salvation can be found in her alone. One of the high points indeed of Michelangelo's art, the image of the virgin repeats the theme of the mother suckling the child. The figure bends with opposing movements, while the face still reflects a noble serenity. The statue was intended to be placed in a niche which was never made. The statues of the two protector *Saints* of the Medici family, like the tomb made for Lorenzo the Magnificent and his brother, Giuliano, were left unfinished. Michelangelo himself entrusted them to two of his pupils, Montorsoli and Raffaele da Montelupo (1505-1566/67).

Finally we come to a small room to the left of the altar. Here, drawn on the wall and mainly the work of Michelangelo, are preparatory drawings and practice designs for the sculptures and other works in the church of San Lorenzo. These were discovered in a cellar under the apse during some maintenance work in 1975. Now, protected behind glass, they provide a fascinating insight into the creative phases and the evolution of ideas by the great master.

View of the chapel vault and cupolas.

CATHEDRAL
MUSEUM

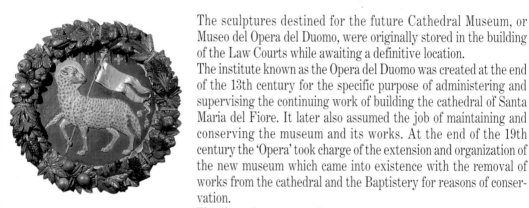

The sculptures destined for the future Cathedral Museum, or Museo del Opera del Duomo, were originally stored in the building of the Law Courts while awaiting a definitive location.

The institute known as the Opera del Duomo was created at the end of the 13th century for the specific purpose of administering and supervising the continuing work of building the cathedral of Santa Maria del Fiore. It later also assumed the job of maintaining and conserving the museum and its works. At the end of the 19th century the 'Opera' took charge of the extension and organization of the new museum which came into existence with the removal of works from the cathedral and the Baptistery for reasons of conservation.

Previous page: Donatello, Habbakuk.

Andrea della Robbia, Agnus Dei.

Luca della Robbia, processional cross.

The 'Opera' was originally housed in a building behind the site of the cathedral but, at the beginning of the 15th century, it was transferred to the present palazzo, altered by Brunelleschi and decorated by Della Robbia with a lunette and the coat of arms of the Opera, an *Agnus Dei.* The sculptures were left unorganized for a considerable length of time, however, and new acquisitions were simply piled up in confusion. A document of 1818 relates that the marble choir galleries and Luca della Robbia's statues for the altars of Sts. Peter and Paul were "in a room...which had until now been the book-keepers' office". There they were heaped with other sculptures, "unknown to the public and difficult for anyone to see, some of them being hidden behind the booths of the clerks". The present organization of the museum was established some decades later when the choir galleries and other artistic items made for the cathedral were put on display together. The new cathedral museum was opened in 1891 and since then many items of artistic importance have been brought here from public and private gardens in the city, as well as marble items from the exterior of the cathedral, the bell tower and the Baptistery, which had suffered deterioration. The museum was restored after the 1966 flood and the display was modernized. In addition to the sculptures it also houses superb liturgical items and wonderful embroidery work, representing important phases in the development of Florentine arts.

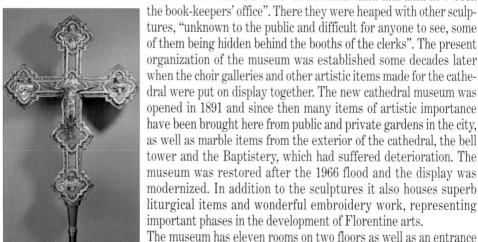

The museum has eleven rooms on two floors as well as an entrance porch and courtyard where busts, tablets, coats of arms, sarcophagi and fragments of classical art are displayed. In the entrance hall is a bust of Filippo Brunelleschi by Baccio Bandinelli, one of the founders of the institution, and a 16th-century baluster from the choir of the cathedral. The first rooms, organized in 1977, are known as the *Sale Brunelleschiane*. These contain wooden models showing the methods used in the building of the cathedral dome and the crowning lantern, completed respectively in 1434 and 1461. There are also carpentery tools used in this immense job and the funeral mask of Filippo Brunelleschi. Next is the *Sala dell'Antica Facciata* with works which decorated the old façade before it's demolition in 1587. To the right, a 16th-century drawing illustrates the arrangement of the façade. Many of the works were saved including a majestic and dignified figure of *St. Luke* (1408-14) by Nanni di Banco (1380/90-1421). This still has some Gothic elements, but these are combined with a more arrogant and expressive self-confidence derived from Donatello. A stylistic comparision can be made here with the *St. John the Evangelist*, (1404-14) by Donatello who defined the realistic and personal characteristics with greater force. Both pieces were made for the low niches on either side of the main door of the cathedral. The group of the *Madonna and Child* which, with *Sts. Reparata* and *Zenobius*, were positioned above the central door of the Duomo, are by Arnolfo di Cambio (c.1245-1302). This is one of the greatest works by Arnolfo who is rightly considered to be one of the greatest masters and creators of Italian art, along with Cimabue and Giotto. The other sculptures which made up the the original decoration of the faáade are also by Arnolfo and workshop. The theme of the glorification of the Virgin, was reconstructed in neo-medieval style by the architect De Fabris in the late 19th century.

Arnolfo di Cambio, Madonna and Child.

Decorated initial in a choir book.

Displayed on the right are models of various ideas which were proposed for the rebuilding of the cathedral façade, such as the plans by Bernardo Buontalenti, Giambologna and Giovanni de' Medici. Opened in 1954, the *Sala dei Corali* once housed part of the Opera's archives. Four choir books are now displayed here. These are some of the 58 beautiful illuminated choir books belonging to the cathedral. They were brought here for better care and maintenance and were displayed, open at the most beautiful pages. In the 1966 flood however, these were unfortunately swept away and, except for these four examples, are now being restored in specialized workshops. Opposite are some examples of religious art and embroidered fabrics, such as the *Chasuble* of cardinal Alessandro Farnese and a large 15th-century *Processional Cross*. Brought here in November 1994 and displayed opposite the entrance is the painting of *Dante with the Divine Comedy* (1465), by Domenico di Michelino (1417-1491) designed by Alessio Baldovinetti. The work was commissioned by the Opera to celebrate the second centenary of the birth of Dante.

We come next to the *Ottagono delle Oreficerie*, housing precious

reliquaries of the 13th to the 18th century. Of particular beauty are the Reliquary of St. Reparata made of partially gilded silver, with engraved medallions; two reliquaries containing parts of a finger of St. John the Baptist, made in burnished silver, and decorated with pierced work and enamels, and the *reliquary* in the form of an ark with little statues of angels on the four corners of the lid, containing St. Peter's chains.

Half way up the stairs leading to the first floor is a statue of the *Pietà* (1550-1555) by Michelangelo. This was one of his last sculptural works, made for the altar of his own chapel in Santa Maria Maggiore in Rome. It was, however, sold for 200 'scudi' to Francesco Bandini who placed it in his gardens in Rome. It probably remained there until 1674, when Cosimo III had it brought to Florence. It was then placed in the crypt of the church of San Lorenzo, but in 1722 it was transferred to the cathedral, first placed behind the main altar though moved in 1933 to the first chapel on the right in the north tribune. It was only recently brought to the museum. This is a sublime and highly expressive work despite the unhappy addition of the Magadalen, for which his pupil, Tiberio Calcagni (1532-1265), was partly responsible. This does not, however, dimminish the vital energy and tragedy expressed in the contorted movement and Michelangelo's famous 'non-finito' style.

Off the landing is the large *Sala delle Cantorie*, named after the two magnificent marble choir galleries by Donatello and Luca Della Robbia. These were originally above the doors to the cathedral sacristies. They were removed and replaced with larger wooden ones in 1688 on the occasion of the marriage of Ferdinando de' Medici, son of Grand Duke Cosimo III, to Violante di Baviera.

Donatello, choir gallery.

Donatello's *choir gallery*, begun in 1433 is on the right. Although it is composed of elements clearly derived from classical sources, its form and style are modern. The unrestrained movement of the dancing putti, the unusual mosaic decoration and the variously coloured marble give the work an air of unrestrained impetuousness.

Luca della Robbia, choir gallery.

The organization of Luca Della Robbia's *choir gallery* (1433-39) is diametrically different. He divided it into a classical framework of squares containing the putti who sing and dance decorously. In this atmosphere of graceful joy Luca della Robbia provides a new interpretation of space, as too did Ghiberti and Donatello. Not controlled entirely by the rules of perspective, it is the result of a gradual sculptural evolution which almost seems to create a three-dimensional image.

Also in this room, beneath Donatello's choir, is his wooden sculpture

of the *Magdalen* (1453-1455). This work was badly damaged in the flood of the 4th November 1966. Today, however, it has been restored to its original colours, previously hidden beneath dark and dull, monochrome over-painting, probably done in the early 19th century. The piece has thus assumed a new meaning: light entirely invigorates the material, representing life instead of the darkness of death. The sixteen other statues in this room came from the niches of the campanile. Especially interesting are *Habbakuk* and *Jeremiah* by Donatello (1426 or 1432), both clothed in flowing robes, with pronounced deep or flattened folds, and *St. John the Baptist* now attributed to Nanni di Bartolo (active 1419-1451). One of the most lovely works by Andrea Pisano (c.1290-after 1348) is the fourth prophet on the right wall.

On the left is the *Sala delle Formelle*, named for the panels which decorated Giotto's campanile, now substituted by copies. They are arranged here in the same order as that on the campanile. The themes represented in these hexagonal panels are those of the arts, sciences and crafts, while in the upper row of diamonds are the planets, the virtues, the liberal arts and the holy sacraments. Twenty-one of the panels are by Andrea Pisano, designed by Giotto, and the other five, with the liberal arts, are by Luca della Robbia. Originally these were coloured, like the background of the diamonds, which still have their original enamel tesserae.

Leaving this room we come to the *Sala dell'Altare*. Housed here are some 14th- and 15th-century Tuscan panel paintings and a series of magnificent panels embroidered in silk and gold, with scenes from the *Life of St. John the Baptist* (1466-80), designed by Antonio del Pollaiolo. The material and colours were extremely faded, but have recently been restored to their original brillance. The twenty-seven square panels in gold and coloured silk made up the decorated, ornamental parts of religious vestments. According to liturgical custom, these consisted of two cassocks, a chasuble and

Donatello, St. John

Luca della Robbia, choir gallery (detail).

Donatello, Mary Magdalen.

Andrea Pisano, panels from Giotto's bell tower.

a cope. Given the iconographic scope, the quality of the composition and use of space, the delicacy of design and the fine execution, these embroideries represent the most important Florentine, narrative cycle of the second half of the 15th century.

In the centre of the room are the four gilded bronze *panels* commissioned in 1425 from Ghiberti for the Baptistery Door of Paradise. Although already restored in 1940, they have recently been subjected to a special treatment to prevent the corrosion of the bronze and thus the loss of the gold leaf. We now see them here in all their splendour and copies have been placed in the Baptistery door. Ghiberti and his assistants were supreme masters of perspective and composition. On a slender strip of bronze, he composed an almost perfect orchestration of the *Stories from the Old Testament* and the use of light and colour lend a pictorial quality to the relief panels. At the end of the room is the *Dossale di St. Giovanni*, or the *Baptistery Altar*, in gilded and enamelled silver. From the late-Gothic period onwards (records give the date of 1366) various great Florentine masters worked on it, until Pollaiolo and Verrocchio took over the work during the Renaissance. The style is typically late 14th-century. In the upper part, pillars decorated with tabernacles lighten the structure and squares in high relief with the *Stories of St. John the Baptist* decorate the bands. The central niche contains an elegant statue by Michelozzo. The various parts of the altar are attached to a wooden frame and the whole is mounted on an inlaid and gilded wooden base topped with a matching frame.

Above the altar is the famous *Cross* in embossed silver laminate, decorated with translucent enamel, made by Antonio del Pollaiolo, Betto di Francesco (active 1457-59) and Bernardo Cennini (c.1415-1498). This was originally intended to be a reliquary for a fragment of the *Holy Wood*, a relic from the piece of the cross brought to Florence from Constantinople in 1459. Pollaiolo succeeded in combining traditional goldsmith's techniques with both a rapid, crisp style and Donatello's sense of space and light thus creating a work of rare decorative and sculptural beauty.

Roman sarcophagus (detail).

The St. John silver altar frontal.

Following page: Michelangelo, Pietà.

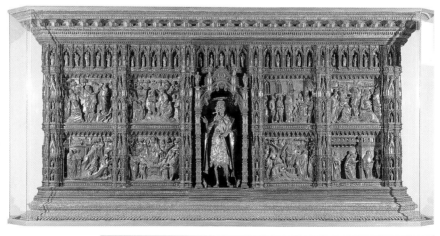

FLORENTINE HOUSE MUSEUM

Previous page: the Chatelaine's Room in Palazzo Davanzati.

Sala dei Pappagalli.

Palazzo Davanzati, now a domestic museum, was built by the Davizzi family in the mid-14th century. It was later sold to the Bartolini family and in 1578 was bought by the well-known historian and writer, Bernardo Davanzati in whose family it remained until the mid-19th century. In 1904 it became the property of the antiquarian, Elia Volpi, who restored its original structure and furnishings. In 1951 it was acquired by the Italian state and opened to the public in 1956 after repair work, mainly to the 14th-century wall decorations damaged by the explosion of bombs on the Santa Trinità bridge during the second World War. The exhibits include furniture, paintings, tapestries, maiolica, embroidery, wall-coverings and domestic articles.

Since 1975 the museum direction has adapted the exhibition space to contemporary requirements and has promoted many cultural and didactic initiatives, intended to develop an interest in and knowledge of the applied arts. Particular attention has been paid to the acquisition, conservation and display of embroidery and lace. Several collections which have been donated to the state illustrate the various techniques and different kinds of Italian and European manufacture.

The building is a fine example of a 14th-century town house, midway between a medieval tower and a Renaissance palace. It consists of four floors of diminishing height, defined by cornices containing five single-light windows with low arches. The original crenellation was replaced in the 16th century by a covered roof-terrace. The three arches of the ground floor loggia are now closed by large doorways. In the centre of the façade is a large 16th-century coat of arms of the Davanzati family, with a *lion rampant*.

The entrance hall has a cross-vaulted ceiling. The porticoed courtyard is overlooked by the galleries of the four floors and was designed to be separate from the exterior. On the walls are fragments of Florentine 15th- and 16th-century frescoes taken from various noble Florentine houses. To the right of the entrance is a well with a bucket attached to a pulley system which served all the floors of the palace.

A steep flight of stairs, in stone up to the first floor and thereafter in wood, leads to the first landing with, on the right a bright *Salone Madornale*. This room, with its beautiful painted wooden ceiling was only used on special occasions. Displayed here are seats, a 16th-century table, and on a cupboard inlayed with a geometric design is a marble *Bust of a Young Boy* by Antonio Rosellino (1427-1478/81), a fine example of a private portrait commission of the mid-15th century. On one side is a Tuscan arms cupboard in Sienese style, painted at the beginning of the 16th century with coloured grotesques, while on the other are two tapestry panels of the same period with decorations woven in silver, gold and silk.

The door on the right of the room leads to the exhibition space created in 1981 for the *Collection of Lace and Embroidery* covering the period from the mid-16th to the 19th century. The pieces are displayed temporarily and changed regularly due to the fragile nature of the material which cannot be exposed to the light for long periods. The clothing of the people portrayed in the paintings around the walls illustrates the use of the items exhibited.

Returning to the previous room and taking the door to the left, we come to the dining room, or the *Sala dei Pappagalli* (parakeets) named after the birds seen in the diamonds of the painted wall decoration, designed to give the warm impression of a draped cloth. One of the most attractive pieces of furniture here is the later 16th-century Tuscan walnut sideboard, decorated with grooved and tapering pilasters and carved shelves, with corners rounded off by

Kitchen on the third floor.

Carved and decorated chest.

frames and niches and base with a convex profile. All these typically 16th-century elements enhance the overall shape of the piece. In the display cases are numerous enamelled terracottas, mainly of central Italian provenance (14th to 15th century).

On the left is a small room containing many interesting items, such as the metal strong-box with grotesques engraved on it, and a Moorish decoration imitating fabric. The coffer was probably made in the workshops of the Florentine armoury, however. In the middle of the room is a particularly interesting 16th-century walnut cabinet with a flap and a series of secret drawers inside. Also of note is the panel painting by Francesco Grannaci (1439-1543) depicting *Joseph lead into Prison* which, together with panels by Andrea del Sarto, Pontormo and Bachiacca (1494-1557), decorated the bridal chamber of a palace in nearby Borgo Santissimi Apostoli.

Returning to the landing, we come to the *Peacock Room*, which takes its name from the coloured decoration of the upper frieze around the four walls painted with a false wall covering. Painted inside the trefoiled arches, are shields containing the coats of arms of some of the most important Florentine families, as well as royal, civic and noble emblems. The bed is Tuscan workmanship of the second half of the 17th century, though it is called 'Genoa style' due to its unusual decoration. The scroll at the head is surmounted by a pediment of dolphins and coats of arms, in a style similar to that of Perin del Vaga. The doors of the tabernacle were painted by Neri di Bicci, a 15th-century artist who still painted in a style reminiscent of earlier times.

Tuscan terracotta for everyday use.

Bedroom with canopied bed and cradle.

Before leaving the first floor one should note the hygenic arrangements. These were a luxury which only the most noble and wealthy houses furnished with tubs, hip-baths, jugs and showers could permit themselves.

On the second floor is another *Sala Madornale* with a 17th-century genealogical tree of the Davanzati family. The last large room is known as the *Chatelaine's Room*. It is believed that the beautiful frescoes which decorate it were painted on the occasion of a marriage between the Davizzi and Alberti families. At the top, beneath an arched loggia, is the tragic, chivalric love story of the Chatelaine of Vergi, inspired by a famous French poem of the day. The room is furnished with a 16th-century walnut bed with four columns, reconstructed in the 19th century; a rustic 17th-century cradle and a chest for clothes, sheets and blankets. There are even shoes from Boccaccio's at house at Certaldo.

In the *dining room* is an early 17th-century cupboard. The style is typically Ligurian, with grooved pilasters and capitals, and doors with square or diamond-shaped frames. To the right is a large inlayed cedarwood chest decorated in Indian ink with designs and scenery with architectural backgrounds. Another, smaller chest is inlayed with geometric designs. The collection of five Flemish tapestries on the walls represent the story of David and Bathsheba. Their colour is particularly well preserved. In the next room are

some small 14th- and 15th-century Tuscan panel paintings with
gold ground by Rossello di Jacopo Franchi (1376-1450) and Spinello
Aretino. The decorations painted by Giovanni di Ser Giovanni,
known as 'Lo Scheggia', are of particular interest. They were
probably made for two wedding chests, now reconstructed, consisting of six parts illustrating Petrarch's 'Triumphs'. The four remaining pieces are the Triumphs of love, death, fame and eternity.

The kitchen is on the third floor, a reminder that these rooms were
generally outside the house itself, or on the upper floors, close to
the roof, so that smoke and smells could escape more easily and also
to reduce the risk of fire. The exhibits here are most interesting: as
well as the fireplace which was the heart of the kitchen, are the
stone sink and the pots, pans and utensils commonly used in
kitchens from the 16th to the 18th century. There are warmers and
centrifugal colanders, mixers and polenta makers, fruit squeezers
and spits. At the end of the room there is also an interesting collection of tools for weaving and embroidery.

Finally, in a room next to the *Sala Madornale* are two Sienese
angel candle-holders (15th-century) in painted wood, an iron
strong-box, also Sienese, from the hospital of Santa Maria Nuova
and an unusual 15th-century Tuscan tabernacle frame in gilded
wood with a blue background.

Bedroom with walnut bed.

Decorated chest.

MICHELANGELO MUSEUM

Daniele da Volterra and Giambologna, bust of Michelangelo.

Following page: Michelangelo, Madonna of the Stairs.

The Casa Buonarroti, housing some important works by Michelangelo, was opened to the public in 1859 when, in accordance with the wishes of the remaining members of the family, it became a charitable institution.

In 1508 Michelangelo bought three small inter-connecting appartments in Via Ghibellina and between 1546-1553 his nephew, Leonardo, built the palace. In 1612 it was altered and given its present structure by Michelangelo Buonarroti the Younger (1568-1647). The last member of the family, Cosimo, left the building to the city on his death in 1858 and in 1859 it was opened to the public as a museum, housing the Buonarroti family's collections of art and archeology.

In 1965 the museum became the 'Casa Buonarroti', exhibiting some of Michelangelo's works of art as well as the family's history and collections. It also hosts temporary exhibitions. The museum contains one of the most important collections of the artist's drawings.

The display is arranged in twenty-one rooms on two floors. On the ground floor is a sculpture, previously attributed to Michelangelo; paintings of the Casa Buonarroti; portraits of Michelangelo and a valuable collection of Etruscan antiquities, sketches and Roman sculptures. The other rooms contain various Renaissance paintings representing the tastes and preferences of the young Michelangelo, maiolica, small Della Robbia sculptures and mineralogical and numismatic collections.

The most interesting works however, are those of the great artist. The first, in Room 11, is the *Battle of the Centaurs*, (before 1492). The mythological theme of this marble sculpture is clearly representative of 15th-century culture, but the experimentation of the 'non-finito' style is innovative. Next is the *Madonna of the Stairs* (1490-92), an early and most original work, although much influenced by Donatello. Room 18, the *Gallery*, was built by Michelangelo the Younger to commemorate his famous great-uncle. It is one of the most interesting 17th-century Florentine collections. On the walls and ceiling are paintings by the most important Florentine painters of the day, glorifying Michelangelo's life and achievements. In the following room, Room 19, is Michelangelo the Younger's study. Lastly, in the Library are some sketches by Michelangelo.

SANTA CROCE MUSEUM

Façade, church of Santa Croce.

The Franciscan monastery of Santa Croce was built at the beginning of the 14th century and the six rooms of the museum are in part of the original structure.

The museum of the church of Santa Croce was opened on 2nd November, 1900 and from 1952 until 1959 it was closed for extensive internal and external restoration. However, the flood of the 4th November 1966 caused extremely severe damage to the building; many of the works were removed for restoration and the rooms were again altered.

In the first room of the museum, the Great Refectory, is the work of art most symbolic of the destruction caused by the flood: Cimabue's *Crucifixion*. This was made about 1280 for the church of Santa Croce and was, in the course of time, displayed in various parts of the basilica and monastery. In the late 13th century the work was representative of a new style of Italian painting, abandoning the solemn and abstract models typical of Byzantine culture. Restoration of the cross was long and extremely complex, but new scientific techniques were developed specifically for this difficult case, thus stimulating vitally important progress in the field of art restoration.

Above the entrance doors in the Refectory are two lunettes by Taddeo Gaddi (1295/1300-1366) and Maso di Banco (active 1341-1346). Displayed on the walls are fourteen tondos and six frescoes with various different subjects, attributed to Andrea Orcagna and his workshop.

On the far wall is a large fresco by Taddeo Gaddi. This was detached for restoration and illustrates the *Tree of the Cross*, the *Last Supper*, and *Scenes from the Life Jesus and the Saints*.

In a niche on the left wall is a gilded bronze statue of *St. Louis of Toulouse*, made by Donatello for the niche of the Guelph faction in Orsanmichele in 1424. It was subsequently moved to the external and later internal faáades of Santa Croce. The saint is portrayed extremely young, gently ecstatic, forgetful of his Bishop's solemnity, timidly raising his hand in benediction.

The fresco of *Sts. Francis and John the Baptist*, removed from the

Cimabue, Crucifix and detail.

Cavalcanti chapel on demolition in 1566, is by Domenico Veneziano. Housed in the Small Refectory, or the Winter Refectory, are fragments of the original stained glass church windows, partially attributed to Giotto and pupils. One wall is entirely covered by a fresco of *St. Francis Distributes Bread to the Monks* by Jacopo Ligozzi. This almost entirely monochrome work was detached, restored and replaced here after the flood.

The third room, previousy the *Cerchi Chapel*, now houses various glazed terrcottas by the Della Robbia family. There are also two fragments of frescoes which were found under the floor of the church after the flood, datable to the mid-13th century.

In a small corridor is another detached fresco, by the workshop of Andrea del Castagno. From here we reach the fourth room with two interesting *Busts of Saints and a capital*, drawn on a wall in black and removed from the Pazzi chapel. Though the attribution is uncertain, it may be a rare painting by Donatello.

The next room contains two lovely sculptures by Tino da Camaino (c.1275-1337), the *Madonna Annunciate* and the *Monument to Cardinal Gastone Della Torre*.

In the last room, as well as a synopsis of a fresco by Jacopo Ligozzi for the Small Refectory, is a *Ciborium* in metal and coloured marble, made by Matteo Nigetti, a late 17th-century Florentine artist. This formed part of the altar in the Castellani Chapel, demolished in 1973.

SANTA MARIA NOVELLA MUSEUM OF SACRED ART

Façade, church of Santa Maria Novella.

The museum is in the rooms previously occupied by the Ubriachi Chapel and the Refectory. It houses a large collection of liturgical items previously kept in the sacristy.

The collection of antique liturgical items belonging to Santa Maria Novella was frequently dispersed and subsequently replaced in the past, but it never succeeded in regaining the splendour and wealth of its early period.

Until the mid-16th century it was enriched by many acquisitions, both donated by private citizens and commissioned by various priors of the monastery. Much of the liturgical clothing was also lost as they were traditionally burnt when no longer fit for wear, to avoid them being used for profane purposes.

All the vestments and altar frontals in the museum are made of rare materials in liturgical colours and have floral decorations contrasting with the background.

This important Museum of Sacred Art was created by the Dominican monks of the church of Santa Maria Novella.

The oldest items are displayed in the first room, the chapel of the Ubriachi family. In the case on the right are two Sienese polychrome wood *Reliquary Busts.*

Made towards the end of the 14th century they are decorated with fine relief work and are inlayed and gilded. They both have a particularly smooth appearance which lends them an air of tranquil peacefulness. The base is decorated with small trefoil arches. The *Relic of the Cross* (a fragment from the INRI inscription on the cross of Christ) is kept in a case of rock crystal, probably Venetian.

In display case B is a charming *Christ Child* in enamelled terracotta, traditionally attributed to Donatello, but more probably by the school of Verrocchio in the mid-15th century. Next is the *St. Catherine of Siena Reliquary*, a skilful composition of various pieces including embossed, gilded and polished copper, enamel and glass, made at different times and by various Florentine and Sienese goldsmiths. Also interesting is the *St. Jerome Reliquary*, which contained fragments of Christ's crown of thorns. The

container and the base are early 15th century, while the mounting of the case containing the relic of St. Jerome is early 17th-century. Opposite is the large *altar frontal* made for the main altar of Santa Maria Novella, dedicated to Our Lady of the Assumption. This was made about 1425 by Paolo Uccello and illustrates the themes of the *Creation of the Animals*, and the *Creation of Adam*, the *Earthly Paradise* and the *Creation of Eve and Original Sin*. Above this display case are the synopses of the frescoes detached from the walls of this chapel, while on the other walls are frescoes of thirty-five prophets, attributed to Orcagna. The paintings on the walls in the second room, the Refectory, are by Agnolo Gaddi and Alessandro Allori. In the first case on the right are religious vestments given to the church in 1656 for the altar dedicated to St. Thomas of Canterbury. The cassocks, the stole, the chasuble and the maniple, of Florentine manufacture, are in silk velvet embroidered with silver thread and lamé and Florentine gold. The techniques used are quilting and appliqué. The chasuble and the cassocks bear the coats of arms of the Minerbetti family who donated the items. This case also contains the *Reliquary Busts of Sts. Anastasia and Mary Magdalen*, made in Lucca by the workshop of Matteo Civitali (1436-1501) at the end of the 15th century.

In the case opposite are a cross by Antonio Mazinghi and the *Processional Cross*, altered in the early 19th century by Gaetano Guadagni, who inserted the copper halo and the emblem of Santa

Maria Novella. In the same case are a reliquary casket, a late 17th-century jug and a large *St. Domenico Reliquary*. Also of interest is the *St. Sebastian Reliquary* (1616) in gilded bronze. The arrow clearly refers to the martyrdom of the saint and the fingers are seen opening in a spasm of pain.

Displayed in case F, beside the *St. Thomas Reliquary* is a partially gilded silver goblet. Although decorated in typically Mannerist style, it is of a later date.

The *Reliquary of the Cross* (1622) is decorated with rubies and has a gilded brass base with two little silver putti. The thorns of Christ's crown which previously were in *St. Jerome's Reliquary* are now kept here. Especially lovely is the 18th-century chased and polished reliquary with a silver statue of the *Virgin and Child*. The style is typically northern European.

The *St. Rossore Reliquary* (1667) was made in Lucca by the Dutch goldsmith, Giovanni Vambrè. The dotted design of small flowers on the sleeve of the relic is a typically late Baroque, Dutch motif. Case G contains three splendid copes.

These articles were originally worn during religious processions for protection from the rain. All three are in quite different materials, colours, styles and techniques and are therefore probably also of different periods. In case H is an early 18th-century cassock in red damask brocade.

Despite the 'bizarre' design of oriental origin, it is either of French or Italian making. Still on the wall to the right are the cases containing the entire set of *San Domenico Vestments*. This is the only set complete with altar frontals remaining in Santa Maria Novella. Beside is a smaller case containing two chasubles with their matching stoles, a maniple and veil, all made in Tuscany in the 19th-century.

Opposite is a collection of silver sacristy items, commissioned or donated between 1816 and 1866, and all made in Florence. Some of these pieces are in Empire style and are attributed to the *Paolo Uccello, fresco in the* Guadagni workshop.

'Choistro verde'.

BARDINI MUSEUM

The Museum houses the collection of Stefano Bardini, an antiquarian and art dealer of international repute during the last century. In 1881 he bought the palace from the bankrupt Mozzi family, together with the adjoining church of San Gregorio della Pace (13th century), with the intention of housing his vast collection of antiques here. Bardini restored the façade and rebuilt the small piazza, bringing more light to the interior, and turned the second floor into a deposit and the top floor into restoration and photographic workshops.

In 1922 Bardini died, having previously decided to leave the entire building and his prestigious collection to the city of Florence.

From the large entrance hall, we enter the room on the right containing a *Bust of St. John the Baptist*, by Andrea Sansovino (1460-1529) though it has also been attributed to Andrea Ferrucci (1465-1526). The work is dated at the beginning of the 16th century.

Continuing in this direction, Room 2 contains ancient Roman pieces, mainly copies of Greek originals. Room 10 is reached up some small steps on the left. Housed here are items recovered during the various phases of demolition which took place in the old city centre during the 19th century. As well as a 15th-century *Tabernacle*, possibly by Andrea Della Robbia, is an *Altarpiece* portraying the *Holy Trinity* inside a circular shield (c.1450) attributed to Michelozzo di Bartolomeo (1397-1472) which may have been part of the altar of the church of Santissima Annunziata. Some critics however disagree with the attribution and believe it may instead have been a baptismal font or a basin, copied from classical sculpture. Also in this room is a beautiful *Madonna and Child* by the workshop of Donatello, two *Angel Candelholders* by Giovanni Della Robbia, and two *Angels in Prayer*, from northern Italy.

At the top of the main staircase we come to the *Sala delle Armi*, where a less well-known aspect of Bardini's collectionism is displayed. This consists of suits of armour, decorated shields and, in particular, an interesting collection of 19th-century pistols. The

Donatello, Madonna and Child.

Lion bearing a column.

most prestigious work of art in Room 14 is without doubt the beautiful *Madonna with Child and Angels* in polychrome plaster by Donatello. The iconography of the piece is rather unusual: five angels play with fine cords, one of which is held by the Virgin.

Room 16 is to the right of the entrance hall. Here are various examples of 14th- and 15th-century art as well as a series of decorated terracottas representing the *Virgin and Child*, all early 15th-century of various origins, and finally a large *Crucifix* by a pupil of Bernardo Daddi.

Above a typical 15th-century Tuscan sacristy cupboard, is a famous painting by Domenico Tintoretto (1560-1635), the *Martyrdom of St. Christina*. The work is distinguished from that of the artist's more famous father, Jacopo, by a lesser degree of emotional and expressive detail and a more narrative element. On the far wall is a beautiful pietra serena *Tabernacle* decorated with candelabra and flowers, dated 1478. It is believed that it originally belonged to the Guild of Doctors and Chemists and that it contained a figure of the Virgin, the emblem of the guild.

Room 15 contains 15th- and 16th-century furniture as well as valuable hangings, coffers and chests. Particularly beautiful is the tempera of *Hercules at the Crossroads* by Domenico Beccafumi painted for the front of a chest. Displayed in one case here are items of gilded wood, terracotta and papier-maché, all 15th-century. Another contains 14th-and 15th-century bronze liturgical items and a 16th-century *cross* in rock-crystal. In the corner opposite is a third case with polychrome terracottas by Giovanni della Robbia and workshop, such as *Judith*, and *Plenty* or *Abundance*. The series of detached frescoes with mythological subjects by Giovanni da San Giovanni and Volterrano (1611-1689), is also of considerable interest. The painting of *Apollo flaying Marsyas* (c.1678) by the Neapolitan painter, Luca Giordano, is also 17th-century. This work is a magnificent example of Caravaggio's realistic style which dominated the 17th century.

In Room 17, as well as important examples of 15th-century art are four *Lion Standard Holders*, wooden sculptures in the Italian Gothic style (c.1300). In the middle of Room 18 is a most beautiful *Madonna Annunciate*, most probably a Sienese work, given the marked tendancy towards a pureness of form and the characteristic lengthening of the body. Above the fireplace is one of Stefano Bardini's most important acquisitions, *St. Michael and the Dragon* (1460-70) by Antonio Pollaiolo, a work referred to by Vasari.

A highly-decorated, 16th-century doorway leads us into the *Musical Instrument Room*, containing an important collection of drawings. There are works of extremely high quality by both Gian Battista Piazzetta (1683-1754) and Gian Battista Tiepolo (1696-1770). The most famous work by Tiepolo is that of the *Holy Family*, a theme frequently illustrated by the artist in various ways. From Room 18 a spiral staircase leads us down into Room

20. In the centre is a large 15th-century polychrome *Crucifix*, probably the work of a Venetian artist in the style of Brunelleschi and Donatello. On the left is another late 13th-century panel painting of the *Crucifixion* by the Maestro di Varlungo. In the middle of the wall on the left are beautiful 15th-century, Tuscan choir stalls, suitably paired by the large choir book on the other side of the room which is also 15th-century. Also in this room are two *Nativities* by the circle of Donatello, in polychrome stucco. This subject was extremely popular in Florence in the 15th century and there are therefore many versions of it in existance. A steep staircase leads us back to the museum entrance where there is a lovely *Charity* (1311-23) by Tino da Camaino. It is believed that the work was made for the chapel of St. Ranieri in Pisa cathedral, for which Tino also made the baptismal font.

Andrea della Robbia, Altarpiece.

Luca Giordano, Apollo flaying Marsyas.

STIBBERT MUSEUM

View of one of the rooms.

Fredrick Stibbert (1838-1906) was a wealthy Anglo-florentine, with a Scottish father and Florentine mother. During his life he collected a vast quantity of arms, paintings, fabrics and other items in his villa and on his death the British government left the inheritance to the city of Florence, thus creating the Stibbert Museum and Foundation. The first complete organization of the material was undertaken in 1883, when the rooms were arranged according to the type of article displayed.

The architecture and internal decor of the villa were undertaken by the best-known members of the Florence Accademia: Giuseppe Poggi, Cesare Fortini, Gaetano Bianchi and Annibale Gatti. The beautiful English-style garden is enhanced with elements which are typical of late 19th-century eclecticism such as little temples, grottos and small loggias.

At the top of the stairs to the left we come to the *Malachite Room*, named after the Empire-style table in the centre made by Philippe Thomire with a top in malachite. The room also houses Etruscan artefacts dating from the 4th century B.C. and Italic items of the 2nd century B.C. In the adjoining rooms are Flemish and French paintings, some 18th-century musical instruments and two splendid chests, one of which is Dutch 17th-century and inlayed with mythological figures, while the other is Italian 16th-century, inlayed with grotesques.

In room V is a large collection of 16th-century suits of armour, of various origin and intended for different purposes such as war, jousting and tournaments. Among the exhibits on the right is an Italian piece, dated about 1560-90, used by horseback riders in tournaments, with a visored helmet, while the left arm, always the most exposed, is heavily protected.

In the *Arms Room* is the famous *Cavalcade*, a collection of European arms, armour and protection for horses. The collection already existed when Stibbert died, but it was arranged in a most dispersive fashion and was only brought together in this way at the beginning of the 1950's. Displayed in a case are various kinds of firearms, from revolver mechanisms to shotguns. These are mainly Italian. The drawing room is decorated with three 16th-century Brussels tapestries and some 15th- and 16th-century painted chests. In a case above the fireplace is a light helmet with three crests, a fine example of Italian embossed decoration used on late 16th-century armour. Of the same period is the suit of armour made up of various fixed basic elements with additional pieces which could be added or removed according to need.

In the next rooms are late Gothic chests from the French-Piedmont area, more armour, European dress swords and bayonets. In the ceiling of Room XIV is an allegorical sketch by Gian Battista Tiepolo. In the passageway and in room XVII are some portraits including one of Alessandro Farnese. In the upper part of the late 19th-century mirror are the monogram and initials of Fredrick Stibbert. Next are two rooms containing short firearms and long swords, all of high quality. The gallery is eclectic in style and from here we reach the large *Ball Room*. The arrangement of this room dates from the end of the 1930's and displayed in a case are the ornate robes worn by Napoleon when he was crowned King of Italy.

The small tiled room at the end of the gallery is the *Fumoir*: a rare example of late 19th-century taste, somewhere between Eclecticism and Liberty. In the *Dining Room* is a *Magdalen* by Alessandro Allori, while in the *White Room*, inspired by the architecture of Fontainebleau, are swords of various periods and origin. The *Jousting Room* is named after the Romantic model seen here and on the other side of it we enter the *Banner Room*. Of special interest are the *Virgin and Child* by the school of Botticelli; the *Venetian Portrait* thought to be of *Cosmè Tura*, and previously attributed to Schiavone, and a fragment of a *Predella* by Neri di Bicci (1419-1491). On the wall beside the staircase are Brussels tapestries depicting cartoons by Rubens. At the top of the stairs are display cases containing church ornaments, especially goblets, crosses, and reliquaries dating from the 12th to the 17th century. On the walls are panel paintings by Mariotto di Nardo (active 1389-1424), Jacopo Orcagna and Andrea Giusto (active 1424-1450), artists all active at the end of the 14th century and during the first half of the 15th century. In a room to the left are wooden sculptures and figures for decorating the crib.

Room XXXVI houses three large cases containing an extremely interesting collection of religious vestments, dated from the 16th to the 18th century. The fabrics preserved in this and in the following rooms is of a very high standard and constitute one of the most important collections of the kind in Europe. The clothing exhibited here is an excellent portrayal of how men's and women's dress developed during the 18th century, illustrating the various fluctuating forms and styles.

Tapestry, the Meeting of Hannibal and Scipio.

Displayed from here until Room XLV are various articles of clothing, costume portraits, hair and hat-pins, dolls' clothes, gloves and other accessories. Continuing, we come to the bedrooms of Fredrick and Giulia Stibbert and three further rooms where many rare and interesting French and Italian fabrics are preserved. There are also two

Sala della Cavalcata. beautiful clocks: one is decorated with Chinese laquer, dated 1790's; the other is 17th-century with gilded bronze decorations.

Returning to the ground floor we come to the area where Islamic and Turkish warriors, Indian, Chinese, Korean and Japanese weapons are displayed. These collections also include costumes, artefacts, prints and miniatures. Oriental armour is usually lighter than European and consists of small plates and discs linked by iron rings. The decoration is usually minute and is embossed or of very fine inlay.

The next room contains excellent Mameluk, Turkish and Persian pieces from the 15th to the 18th century. In the cases between the windows are long firearms such as the blunderbuss with the characteristically shaped mouth. The next room is entirely white as Stibbert himself ordered and houses arms and costumes mainly from Muslim India. Returning through the Islamic rooms and climbing a spiral staircase, we reach the Japanese rooms with traditional armour as well as masks with ferocious expressions and helmets with strange crests intended to frighten the enemy. In the centre of the adjoining room is a female figure in a Chinese wedding outfit of pink and blue silk with gold and silver embroidery.

HORNE MUSEUM

This museum houses the large and interesting collection of Herbert Percy Horne (1864-1916), an English architect, art critic and man of many interests who lived for many years in Florence. In 1911 he acquired a palazzo in Via dei' Benci which had belonged in the past to the Alberti and Corsi families. In the 1400's it had been rebuilt to a design by Giuliano da Sangallo. Horne restored the building with the idea of creating, not so much a museum, as an example of a nobleman's Renaissance house. In his will he left his collection to the city of Florence.

The wide range of items displayed is in perfect harmony with the setting. The collections of drawings and prints, the archive and the library are of particular importance.

From an inner courtyard we reach the first room where a portrait of Horne seems to welcome us. A large collection of coins (many of them Etruscan, Greek-Italic and Roman), medallions, small plaques, seals, pieces of china and maiolica of various periods and origins is displayed here.

Domenico Beccafumi, Holy Family.

From the courtyard we reach the first floor with a covered balcony. In the first room are small 15th- and early 16th-century panel paintings from Tuscany and Emilia Romagna. In the case on the wall, with other fragments, is a painting of *San Giuliano* by Masaccio. On the far wall are a triptych by Pietro Lorenzetti with *Sts. Benedetto, Caterina d'Alessandria and Margherita*, a *St. Girolamo* by Piero di Cosimo and two small panels with a *Crucifixion* and *Virgin and Child with Saints* by Bernardo Daddi, originally part of a polyptych.

The large *Deposition* by Benozzo Gozzoli was unfinished at the

Room on the first floor. death of the artist. Gozzoli was a pupil of Fra' Angelico and this work fully demonstrates his style of painting which was more modern and more sophisticated than that of his great master. The room is furnished with two fine Renaissance chests and a 17th-century walnut table.

In the second room, on the entrance wall, a tempera panel painting by Domenico Beccafumi illustrates the mythical theme of *Deucalion and Pyrrha*. On the right wall is a beautiful painting of *St. Steven* by Giotto whose modern, more realistic and sculptural style was to influence the great artists of the 15th century. On a table is Giambologna's terracotta model for the *Athlete*, while displayed in a 17th-century cupboard with four doors at the end of the room are jewels, candlesticks and table items from the 16th to the 18th century.

The third room contains mainly 14th- and 15th-century paintings. The tondo of the *Holy Family* by Domenico Beccafumi is, instead, 16th-century. The unusually bright colours are somehow similar to those of Michelangelo's Doni Tondo. Displayed in a case on the table are 15th-century containers for relics, decorated with gilded and inlayed wood and bone. The folding chessboard is also of fine workmanship.

The fourth room is on the second floor, on the left. As well as the rare and beautiful articles and furniture here there are paintings by artists such as Ercole de' Roberti and Filippino Lippi. Between the windows at the far end is a polychrome stucco of the *Madonna of the Candles*, by Antonio Rossellino. The gold decoration gives a vibrant aspect to the light and seems to render the figure truely

three dimensional. Set against the far wall in the fifth room is a small canopied bed of inlayed and carved walnut, made in Florence in the 15th century. To the right of this is the *Drunkeness of Noah* by Beccafumi.

Lastly, in the sixth room are numerous items of daily domestic use, such as watering cans with a tapped spout, 17th- and 18th-century card games, table cutlery and kitchen utensils from various periods and an antique stove. Displayed in one case are tools used by craftsmen, architects and engineers, while in another are tools of the female crafts, including some fine examples in ivory.

Giotto, St. Steven.

MUSEO DELL'OPIFICIO DELLE PIETRE DURE

Medici coat of arms borne by putti.

Grand Duke Ferdinando I first housed the semi-precious stone workshops in the Casino di San Marco in 1588. They were later moved to the Uffizi and there they remained for two centuries until Grand Duke Pietro Leopoldo decided to move them to the building previously occupied by the hospital of San Matteo and the adjoining convent of San Niccolò. The work of rebuilding and transferring the Opificio began in 1790 and continued until 1855 and this small yet fascinating museum was, in fact, opened in the mid-19th century.

In the large courtyard of the Opificio are pieces of stone and marble collected by the Medici from the 16th century onwards for the internal decoration of the Chapel of the Princes in San Lorenzo. Around the courtyard are the workshops and the museum. In the first room the skill of working semi-precious stone is represented by some antique and modern examples in porphery such as the late 17th-century *Medici Coat of Arms Borne by Putti*.

The second room contains items of great importance in the history of the Opificio: the panels once made for the altar of the Medici Dukes' chapel in San Lorenzo. The making of these panels lasted from the beginning of the 17th century until the middle of the 19th century. In the central display case are Cigoli's *Landscapes* in pietradura mosaic. This typically Florentine style of inlay work is a technique which derived from 'sectioned' mosaic work, using pieces of different size cut according to a specific design. It is especially suited to semi-precious stones and silicons such as quartz, agate, chalcedony and jasper. In the third room, with walls decorated in the style of a 19th-century drawing room, is a table by Niccolì Betti, the last piece of furnishing made for Palazzo Pitti.

The fourth room houses examples of 'paintings on stone' and Florentine scagliola. The first is a technique of painting directly on to the stone with a brush which, however, is somewhat fragile and subject to changes in the colour tones with the passing of time. Scagliola, on the other hand, is a process using a plaster base, reinforced with plant fibre to increase the strength and lighten the weight of the panels. The base is then hollowed out where the designs and figures are to be placed, and these are then filled with a paste of scagliola amalgamated with colour pigment. Also in this

Niccolò Betti, *Semi-precious stone mosaic.*

Domenico Remps, *Still life.*

room are many preparatory oil paintings with their corresponding pietra dura panels.

The same comparison between oils and pietre dure can also be seen at the beginning of the next room. Of particular note here is the large *jardinière* in black and white marble, designed by Edoardo Marchionni in 1877. The combination of 'poor' and precious materials makes the work appear somewhat contradictory and unharmonious. However the quality of the design and the subtle colouring of the four panels make this one of Marchionni's finest pieces. On the far wall is a small fireplace in Siberian malachite and gilded bronze. Dated late-19th century, it is of Russian manufacture with French influence. On the same wall is a Ciborium in semi-precious stone with bas-relief. It was commissioned in 1782 by Grand Duke Pietro Leopoldo.

On the other side of the stairway is the sixth room, containing 19th-century pieces. There are circular table tops, picture frames decorated with flowers, writing accessories, necklaces, a book-cover, tobacco jars and various decorative panels. The last room contains almost entirely work-benches with work frames and tools. The cases on the walls display samples of various materials and diagrams of the machines used to work the stone.

Today the Opificio houses a famous restoration workshop and the institute is also renowned for its school and important scientific laboratories.

MARINO MARINI MUSEUM

The church of San Pancrazio, now the Marino Marini Museum, is one of the oldest churches in Florence. Reference to it is found in a document dated AD.931.

In the past the church was frequently restored and rebuilt, until its dissolution in 1808. In the 19th century the building became an administrative office for the lottery, then a military store and later again a state tobacco deposit. It was recently completely restored and in 1988 it opened as a museum to house the works donated to Florence by the sculptor and artist, Marino Marini (1901-1980). The museum is therefore an excellent example of how a disused building can be newly employed, while respecting the original structure. Marini was an esteemed artist of international repute. Born in Pistoia, he attended the Academy of Fine Arts in Florence and devoted himself mainly to painting, influenced by the artistic style known as the 'return to order' which characterized the early decades of this century. At the end of the 1920's, the sculptor, Arturo Martini invited him to Milan to teach at the Villa Reale in Monza. In 1940 he accepted the position of professor of sculpture at the prestigious Academia di Brera.

The museum houses paintings, drawings and sculptures covering a considerable period of time (from the 1920's to the early 1960's), representative of the various phases, interests and influences in Marini's artistic development. The exhibits illustrate, in particular, the continual flow and exchange between painting and sculpture, with painting representing an extension of the stylistic possibilities of sculpture.

Some of the most important works are, for example, the *Man on a Horse*, a polychrome gesso of 1937, on the ground floor. This is an early example of the sculptural prototype which Marini repeated frequently. It is a re-working of the classic Italian *Equestrian Statue* which so impressed Marini in Marcus Aurelius' Capitoline Hill in Rome and again in Padua and Venice in the works of Donatello and Verrocchio.

On the mezzanine is the *Bather*, 1932, a male nude sculpted in wood, with the head resting against the left hand in a reflective pose. Lastly, on the top floor is a group of *Dancers* in a circle.

Venus.

Horseman.

FIRENZE COM'ERA MUSEUM

Giusto Utens, The Medici villa, 'La Peggio'.

The topographical museum of the city came into existence in 1909 when the documentary material which had been acquired and donated by many leading citizens was temporarily arranged in Michelangelo's house in Via Ghibellina. Later, with the creation of the Michelangelo Museum there, the collection was transferred to the monastery of San Marco. In 1955 it was again moved and housed on the first floor of the newly restored Oblate convent. Following re-organization, the collection was displayed in some rooms on the ground floor, where it still is today.

The material consists mainly of prints and paintings of Florence ranging from early medieval items, showing towers and city walls to the picturesque alleys and piazzas of the 19th century.

The first room is to the right of the entrance and displayed here are rare, 15th-century wood engravings by Giovanni Filippo Bergomese and Jacopo Clauser. Opposite the door is a 19th-century tempera copy of the famous *Pianta della Catena* (1470). Of great interest too is the large *Topographical Map of the City* (1584) by Stefano Bonsignori, Duke Francesco I's cosmographer. This is the first perspective representation of the city and its buildings.

In the second room are views by Spada (1576-1622), Werner, Ruggeri (1691-1741) and Zocchi (1711-1767) of the city during the 1600's and 1700's. The geometric plans made between 1843 and 1866 by Federico Fantozzi (c.1803-1865) show the changes made to the urban structure before Florence became the national capital. The watercolours by Giuseppe Maria Terreni (1739-1811) of the celebrations in the Casine park are charming. A collection of small paintings, pastels and etchings by Marani and Telemaco Signorini show some areas characteristic of the old city centre, before the radical programme of re-development at the end of the 19th century. Lastly are some romantic Florentine landscapes by Vanvitelli (1700-1773), Thomas Smith (active in the early 20th century) and Thomas Patch. Displayed in a case are carictures of some famous 19th-century Florentines by the Neapolitan, Melchiorre Defico.

The beautiful lunettes in the salon are decorated with water-

colours representing the *Medici villas* with their parks and gardens, painted in 1599 by the Flemish painter Giusto Utens (active 1558-1609). Also in this room is a collection of drawings donated by the Florentines, Alberto and Lucia Levi, in memory of their mother who was deported and died in a concentration camp. There are splendid paintings from the Ottone Rosai donation (1895-1957), including the *Tondini*, portraits of his contemporaries and the series of the *Friends of Rosai*.

In the middle of the other rooms to the left of the entrance are cases with scenes of Florence (1754) by Giuseppe Zocchi, illustrating buildings, squares, villas and festivals. The last room is dedicated to Giuseppe Poggi (1811-1901), the architect who planned the reorganization of Florence adapting it to its role as national capital. The plans for urban re-structure, some of which were never carried out, and the original route of the Viale dei Colli are exhibited here. The scheme provided for a re-organization of the city centre and the main access roads. A rectangular network of new residential zones was built outside the old city walls which were demolished to make way for the new ring roads. The city gates were retained though, as junction points for the traffic. Many of these plans, however, proved to be inadequate.

Giovanni Signorini, View of Florence.

Following pages: the 'Chain Map'.

BIBLIOGRAPHY

C. Acidini Luchinat (a cura di), *Fiorenza in villa*. Firenze, 1987.

F. Albertini, *Memoriale di molte statue et picture sono nella inclita città di Florentia*. Firenze, 1510.

U. Baldini, *Un Leonardo inedito*. Firenze, 1992.

U. Baldini, *Michelangelo scultore*. Firenze, 1981.

U. Baldini, P.Dal Poggetto, *Firenze restaura*. Firenze, 1972.

P. Barocchi, G.Gaeta Bertelà, *Museo Nazionale del Bargello. Itinerario e Guida*. Firenze, 1984.

L. Becherucci, G.Brunetti, *Il Museo dell'Opera del Duomo*. Voll.2., Milano, 1970.

L. Berti, *Il Museo di San Marco*. Milano, 1961.

L. Berti, *Il Museo di Palazzo Davanzati*. Milano, 1971.

L. Berti, *Gli Uffizi. Catalogo generale*. Firenze, 1980.

L. Berti, *Michelangelo e i disegni di casa Buonarroti*. Firenze, 1985.

L. G. Boccia (a cura di) *Museo Bardini. Le armi*. Firenze, 1985.

G. Bonsanti, *Firenze, l'Angelico al convento di San Marco*. Novara, 1982.

G. Bonsanti, *La Galleria dell'Accademia. Guida e catalogo completo*. Firenze, 1990.

E. Borsook, *Ecco Firenze*. Milano, 1983.

A. Caneva, A.Cecchi, A.Natali, *Gli Uffizi. Guida alle collezioni e catalogo completo dei dipinti*. Firenze, 1986.

F. Cardini, *Breve storia di Firenze*. Pisa, 1990.

O. Casazza, L.Cavallo, *Soffici. Arte e storia*. Milano,1994

Catalogo *Metodo e Scienza. Operatività e ricerca nel Restauro*. Firenze, 1982.

Catalogo *Raffaello a Firenze*. Firenze,1984.

Catalogo *Capolavori e Restauri*. Firenze, 1986.

R. Chiarelli, *San Lorenzo e le Cappelle Medicee*. Firenze, 1989.

M. Chiarini, *Palazzo Pitti*. Firenze, 1988.

M. S. De Salvia Baldini, *Dizionario del gioiello. Lusso e magiche virtù*. Milano,1994

M. S. De Salvia Baldini, *L'abc dell'eleganza. Dizionario dell'abbigliamento*. Milano, 1994.

G. Di Cagno, *Il Duomo, il Battistero e il Campanile*, 1994.

D. Durbé, *I macchiaioli*. Roma, 1978.

M. Fossi Todorow, *Palazzo Davanzati. Museo dell'antica casa fiorentina*. Firenze, 1990.

Guida *Firenze e Dintorni*. T.C.I. Milano, 1993.

M. Gregori (a cura di) *Cappelle barocche a Firenze*. Milano, 1990.

F. Gurrieri, *Boboli Gardens*. Firenze, 1972.

G. L. Maffei, *La casa fiorentina nella storia della città*. Venezia, 1990.

G. Marchini, *Il Battistero e il Duomo di Firenze*. Firenze, 1972.

E. Micheletti, *Firenze. Gli Uffizi*. voll.2. Firenze, 1983.

A. Paolucci, *Il Laboratorio di restauro a Firenze* [L'Opificio delle Pietre Dure]. Torino, 1986.

C. Piacenti Aschengreen, *Il Museo degli Argenti a Firenze*. Milano, 1967.

C. Piacenti Aschengreen, *La Galleria del costume: Palazzo Pitti*. Firenze, 1983-88, 3 voll.

G. Ragionieri, V. E. Vasarri, *Casa Buonarroti*. Firenze, 1987.

F. Rezeto, M.Marini, *Il Museo Archeologico di Firenze*. Firenze, 1985

D. Salvestrini (a cura di), *Guida ai musei della Toscana*. Milano, 1988.

F. Scalia, C. De Benedictis, *Il museo Bardini a Firenze*. Milano, 1984.

M. Scudieri, *Museo di San Marco*. Firenze, 1991

M. Sframeli (a cura di), *Il centro di Firenze restituito*. Firenze 1989

B. Tomasello, *Il museo del Bargello*. Firenze, 1991.

G. Vasari, *Le vite de' più eccellenti architetti, pittori et scultori italiani* (1550), Torino,1970

D. Wigny, *Firenze*. Milano, 1991.